PRAISE FOR
SEX OBJECT

"*Sex Object* is also an antidote to the fun and flirty feminism of selfies and self-help." —*New Republic*

"Yes, All Men (And Everyone Else) Need To Read *Sex Object*." —NPR

"Powerful.... Incredibly readable.... She wants to take us back to a place of telling stories." —*The Nation*

"A bold undertaking.... Consciousness-raising.... [Valenti is] one of America's best-known and often divisive feminists." —*The Guardian* (UK)

"A powerful literary memoir that expertly makes the case for feminism today." —*Harper's Bazaar*

"A zesty, zeitgeisty memoir." —*O, The Oprah Magazine*

"Amazing.... A profoundly raw and honest book." —Ezra Klein, *Vox*

"Jessica Valenti is widely known as a feminist leader—with this stunningly brave and often funny memoir, we get a chance to know her as a human being. This is an incredibly powerful book. I can't recommend it loudly enough." —Jill Soloway, writer, producer, and creator of the Emmy-winning show *Transparent*

SEX OBJECT

SEX OBJECT

A MEMOIR

Jessica Valenti

DEY ST.

An Imprint of William Morrow *Publishers*

HarperCollins books may be purchased for educational, business, or sales promotional use. For information please e-mail the Special Markets Department at SPsales@harpercollins.com.

A hardcover edition of this book was published in 2016 by Dey Street Books, an imprint of William Morrow Publishers.

FIRST DEY STREET BOOKS PAPERBACK EDITION PUBLISHED 2017.

Designed by Ashley Tucker

Library of Congress Cataloging-in-Publication Data has been applied for.

ISBN 978-0-06-243509-5

19 20 21   OV/LSC   10 9 8 7 6

For Layla and Zoe.
If the world is not a different one for you,
I hope you both will change it.
No pressure.

CONTENTS

I am what I am. To look for reasons is beside the point.
—Joan Didion, *Play It as It Lays*

INTRODUCTION

All women live in objectification the way fish live in water.
—Catharine A. MacKinnon

WHEN I WAS A CHILD, I HAD REOCCURRING NIGHTMARES ABOUT wolves—tall beasts the size of skyscrapers that walked on their hind legs around New York City blocks, chasing and eventually devouring me. My mother says she made the mistake of bringing me to see a live performance of *Little Red Riding Hood* when I was a toddler, and that the man dressed as the wolf terrified me. I started having the dreams almost immediately after the play and they lasted well into high school; I don't remember when they stopped.

Over the last few years, as I've dug deeper into my feminism, become an author and a mother, I've found myself thinking about those dreams a lot. It was just a play, just a man in a scary costume—yet my young brain was impacted indelibly.

Given all that women are expected to live with—the leers that start when we've barely begun puberty, the harassment, the violence we survive or are constantly on guard for—I can't help but wonder what it all has done to us. Not just to how women experience the world, but how we experience ourselves.

I started to ask myself: *Who would I be if I didn't live in a world that hated women?* I've been unable to come up with a satisfactory answer, but I did realize that I've long been mourning this version of myself that never existed.

This book is called *Sex Object* not because I relish the idea of identifying as such: I don't do it coyly or to flatter myself. I don't use the term because I think I'm particularly sexy or desirable, though I've been called those things before at opportune moments.

For a long time, I couldn't bear to call myself an author. I've written books, yet the word still felt false rolling off my tongue. The same thing happened when I got married—"wife" seemed alien, but that's what I was, someone's wife. Unlike "author" or "wife," "sex object" was not an identity I chose for myself as much as it was one pushed upon me from twelve years old on; I admit my use of the term is more resignation than reclamation. Still, we are who we are.

I have girded myself for the inevitable response about my being too unattractive to warrant this label, but those who will say so don't realize that being called a thing, rather than a person, is not a compliment. That we might think of it that way is part of the problem.

Being a sex object is not special. This particular experience of sexism—the way women are treated like objects, the way we sometimes make ourselves into objects, and how the daily sloughing away of our humanity impacts not just our lives and experiences but our very sense of self—is not an unusual one. This object status is what ties me to so many others. This is not to say that women all experience objectification in the same way; we do not. For some, those at the margins, especially, it's a more violent and literal experience than I could imagine or explain.

What I know is that despite my years of writing about feminism, I've never had the appropriate language to describe what it has meant to live with these things: The teacher who asked me on a date just a few days after I graduated high school. The college ex-boyfriend who taped a used condom to my dorm room door, scrawling "whore" across my dry-erase board. The Politico reporter who wrote an article about my breasts.

The individual experiences are easy enough to name, but their cumulative impact feels slippery.

A high school teacher once told me that identity is half what we tell ourselves and half what we tell other people about ourselves. But the missing piece he didn't mention—the piece that holds so much weight, especially in the minds of young women and girls—is the stories that *other people tell us about ourselves*. Those narratives become the ones we shape ourselves into. They're who we are, even if so much of it is a performance.

This book is about more than the ways in which I grew up feeling sexually objectified, though—exploring as much would be too pat. The feminism that's popular right now is largely grounded in using optimism and humor to undo the damage that sexism has wrought. We laugh with Amy Schumer, listen to Beyoncé tell us that girls run the world or Sheryl Sandberg when she tells us to *lean in*.

Despite the well-worn myth that feminists are obsessed with victimhood, feminism today feels like an unstoppable force of female agency and independence. Of positivity and possibility.

Even our sad stories, of which there are many, have their takeaway moral lessons or silver lining that allows us to buck up, move on, keep working.

This is not just a survival technique but an evangelizing strategy, and a good one at that. But maybe we're doing ourselves a disservice by working so hard to move past what sexism has done to us rather than observe it for a while.

Maybe it's okay if we don't want to be inspirational just this once.

My daughter, Layla, is shy but fierce. I don't know if it was the circumstances of her birth—born too early and too small, sick for so long—but she is a master in the art of survival and making herself known.

This year, in kindergarten, her class was told they were going to put on a performance of *The Three Little Pigs*. Parts would be given out by teachers, who told the children, *You get what you get and you don't get upset*. And so Layla got her part—the first little pig with the straw house. She was unhappy, and when I reiterated the teacher's rule about fairness and accepting the roles we are cast in she told me clearly: *The only ones I want to be are the pig with the brick house or the wolf.* When I asked her why her answer was simple.

Because I want to be one of the ones who doesn't get eaten.

Now, her answer may have come from a place of fear—fairy tales feel real at this age—but still I was proud. My timid girl will not accept a role in which she will be devoured. She wants to live, to be the one doing the eating. I don't know that I can hope for much more.

I wrote this book because I want her to feel that way always.

When I wrote *Sex Object*, it was with the hope that I could put into words the lifelong feeling that so many women have—this feeling that we are less than, that to the people around us we are little more than the sum of our sexual parts. I wanted to show what this feeling—and the harassment and objectification that cause it—does to a person. How we carry it with us through our lives.

I never could have expected that the response to the book would be so incredible—that I'd hear from so many women eager to talk about the things in their lives that they kept hidden, or ignored, for so long. And, most surprisingly, that I'd hear from so many men. Men who told me they realized sexism existed, they realized women got harassed—but that until reading the book they hadn't realized how unrelenting it was.

And then something amazing happened: #MeToo. Sparked by activists, journalists, and brave women coming forward—

the moment that so many of us had waited for was here. And it's better than we ever imagined.

What's so heartening and exciting about #MeToo is that it's not just a campaign about coming forward to share our traumas and stories—that's just the first step. It's a movement to make people realize that *this is not normal*. It's not normal to go through life girding ourselves for the next violation, not normal to raise our daughters to be watchful and protective. But more that realizing that this isn't normal, this moment is telling the world that this is not acceptable. That we expect more.

That's why some of the most important conversations and debates that are happening right now aren't about Harvey Weinstein or Bill Cosby. Yes, we're talking about rape and serial violent abusers—but we're also talking about something else. About the smaller indignities, the things women used to call "bad sex"—or the things we had no language for.

Because #MeToo is about more than what's legal or illegal—it's about what's right. And while it's true that women are fed up with sexual harassment and violence, it's also true that what this culture considers "normal" sexual behavior is often harmful to women. And that we want that to stop too. True change isn't just about stopping the obvious violations—but about interrogating the way that men are taught to wear women down to acquiesce rather than looking for an enthusiastic yes.

The danger, as it's always been with powerful feminist movements and moments, is the backlash. Already we've seen people claiming that women have gone "too far"—that we're

punishing men too much, or too widely broadening the definition of what assault and harassment mean. The truth, of course,
is that even the men who have admitted to sexual wrongdoing
have not faced severe consequences. No one has gone to jail. A
few have lost their jobs, but far more have kept them. The truth
is that this movement has been far more gentle to abusers than
abusers deserve.

If we had as much concern about women's safety as we do
about men's reputations and jobs, this movement never would
have needed to happen.

Right now, women are asking for more than the bare min-
imum that they've been taught to expect. They're asking for a
standard of behavior from men that sees them as full human
beings rather than sexual objects. We're asking—no, demand-
ing—that our desires and safety are universally accepted in the
way that men's have always been.

It's a project with no end date—not because things are that
bad, but because women are that energized. I know that we
won't stop until there are no more sad and scary stories to tell.

Until then, we work and we share and we make sure that
everyone around us knows the truth. I feel so proud to be in the
company of such brave women.

PART I

She had an inside and an outside now and
suddenly she knew how not to mix them.

—Zora Neale Hurston, *Their Eyes Were Watching God*

LINE VIOLENCE

IT TOOK ME A LONG TIME TO REALIZE I WAS NOT THE ONLY GIRL whose high school teacher asked her on a date. Not the only one who sat on the train across from a man who had "forgotten" to zip his fly on the day he "forgot" to wear underwear so that his penis, still tucked in his jeans, was fully visible. I remember joking about it with my father—the weirdo with his dick showing! He had to explain to me that it wasn't an accident.

I am not the only one who had a boyfriend who called me stupid. Not the only one who grew up being told to be careful around groups of boys, even if they were my friends. When I was twelve—the same year I saw my first penis on a New York City subway platform, two years before I would lose my virginity to a guy from Park Slope who filled in his sideburn gaps with his mom's eyeliner, and six years before I would fail out of college, tired of frat boys taping used condoms to my dorm room door—I started to have trouble sleeping. I felt sick all the time.

I KNOW IT'S CALLED THE CYCLE OF VIOLENCE, BUT IN MY FAMILY, female suffering is linear: rape and abuse are passed down like the world's worst birthright, largely skipping the men and marking the women with scars, night terrors, and fantastic senses of humor.

My mother told me about getting molested by a family friend as part of our "bad touch" talk. She called him her uncle. We were sitting on my twin bed in a room covered with glow-in-the-dark star stickers. She was eight when he came to the house with ice cream, and while her mother cooked dinner in the kitchen he told her to come sit on his lap if she wanted some. She doesn't remember what he touched or how, just that it happened, and that she said nothing afterward. Some time later the neighborhood barber told my grandmother that if my mom would fold some towels for him, her haircut would be free. So my grandmother left while she worked, and he took my mother into the back room, where he rubbed his penis on her eight-year-old body.

When my grandmother was ten, her father died of alcoholism and she went to live with an aunt and uncle. When she was eleven, her uncle raped her. She told her aunt, and was sent to St. Joseph's Orphanage in Brooklyn the next day.

It's losing steam with each generation, so that's something. My grandmother's rape is my mother's molestation is me getting off relatively easy with abusive boyfriends and strangers fondling me on subways—one time without my realizing until I went to put my hands in my jeans' back pockets and there was semen all over them.

My aunts and mom joked about how often it happened to them when they were younger—the one man who flashed a jacket open and had a big red bow on his cock, the neighborhood pervert who masturbated visibly in his window as they walked to school as girls. (The cops told them the man could do whatever he wanted in his own house.) "Just point and laugh," my aunt said. "That usually sends them running."

Usually.

But worse than the violations themselves was the creeping understanding of what it meant to be female—that it's not a matter of *if* something bad happens, but *when* and *how bad*.

Of course what feels like a matrilineal curse is not really ours. We don't own it; the shame and disgust belong to the perpetrators. At least, that's what the books say. But the frequency with which women in my family have been hurt or sexually assaulted starts to feel like a flashing message encoded in our DNA: *Hurt. Me.*

My daughter is five and I want to inoculate her against whatever it is that keeps happening to the women in my family. I want Layla to have her father's lucky genes—genes that walk into a room and feel entitled to be there. Genes that feel safe. Not my out-of-place chromosomes that are fight-or-flight ready.

This is the one way in which I wish she was not mine.

When I was pregnant, I often joked about wanting a boy. A baby girl would turn into a teenage girl, and I remember the young asshole I was to my mother. But this is closer to the truth:

having a girl means passing this thing on to her, this violence and violations without end.

Because while my daughter lives in a world that knows what happens to women is wrong, it has also accepted this wrongness as inevitable. When a rich man in Delaware was given probation for raping his three-year-old daughter, there was outrage. But it was the lack of punishment that seemed to offend, not the seemingly immovable fact that *some men rape three-year-olds*. Prison time we can measure and control; that some men do horrible things to little girls, however, is presented as a given.

Living in a place that has given up on the expectation of your safety means walking around in a permanently dissociative state. You watch these things happen to you, you walk through them on the subway and on the street, you see them on the television, you hear them in music, and it's just the air you breathe, so you narrate the horror to yourself because to engage with it would be self-destruction.

I spoke on a panel once with a famous new age author/guru in leather pants and she said that the problem with women is that we don't "speak from our power," but from a place of victimization. As if the traumas forced upon us could be shaken off with a steady voice—*as if we had actual power to speak from.*

Victimhood doesn't need to be an identity, but it is a product of facts. Some women heal by rejecting victimhood, but in a world that regularly tells women they're asking for it, I don't know that laying claim to "victim" is such a terrible idea. Recognizing suffering is not giving up and it's not weak.

"Something bad happened to me." More accurately: "Someone did something bad to me." This happened. This happens.

When this reality started to become more and more clear to me, as I grew breasts and took subways, watched movies and fucked boys, I didn't make a conscious decision not to lie down and die. But do I know that my survival instinct took over and I became the loudest girl, the quickest with a sex joke, the one who laughed at old men coming on to her. *

If I was going to be a sex object, I was going to be the best sex object I could be. Over twenty years later, I still feel sick. I still can't sleep. But at least now I understand why.

WE KNOW THAT DIRECT VIOLENCE CAUSES TRAUMA—WE HAVE shelters for it, counselors, services. We know that children who live in violent neighborhoods are more likely to develop PTSD, the daily fear changing their brains and psychological makeup so drastically that flashbacks and disassociation become common. We know people who are bullied get depressed and sometimes commit suicide.

Yet despite all these thing we know to be true—despite the preponderance of evidence showing the mental and emotional distress people demonstrate in violent and harassing environments—we still have no name for what happens to women living in a culture that hates them.

We are sick people with no disease, given no explanation for our supposedly disconnected symptoms. When you catch a cold or a virus, your body has ways of letting you know that you are sick—you cough, you get a fever, your limbs literally hurt.

But what diagnosis do you give to the shaking hands you get after a stranger whispers "pussy" in your ear on your way to work? What medicine can you take to stop being afraid that the cabdriver is not actually taking you home? And what about those of us who walk through all this without feeling any of it— what does it say about the hoops our brain had to jump through to get to ambivalence? I don't believe any of us walk away unscathed.

I do know, though, that a lot of us point and laugh. The strategy of my aunts and mother is now my default reaction when a fifteen-year-old on Instagram calls me a cunt or when a grown-up reporter writes something about my tits. Just keep pointing and laughing, rolling your eyes with the hope that someone will finally notice that *this is not very funny*.

Pretending these offenses roll off of our backs is strategic— *don't give them the fucking satisfaction*—but it isn't the truth. You lose something along the way. Mocking the men who hurt us—as mockable as they are—starts to feel like acquiescing to the most condescending of catcalls, *You look better when you smile*. Because even subversive sarcasm adds a cool-girl nonchalance, an updated, sharper version of the expectation that women be forever pleasant, even as we're eating shit.

This sort of posturing is a performance that requires strength I do not have anymore. Rolling with the punches and giving as good as we're getting requires that we subsume our pain under a veneer of *I don't give a shit*. This inability to be vulnerable—the unwillingness to be victims, even if we are—doesn't protect us, it just covers up the wreckage.

But no one wants to listen to our sad stories unless they are smoothed over with a joke or nice melody. And even then, not always. No one wants to hear a woman talking or writing about pain in a way that suggests that it doesn't end. Without a pat solution, silver lining, or happy ending we're just complainers—downers who don't realize how good we actually have it.

Men's pain and existential angst are the stuff of myth and legends and narratives that shape everything we do, but women's pain is a backdrop—a plot development to push the story along for the real protagonists. Disrupting that story means we're needy or selfish, or worst of all, man-haters—as if after all men have done to women over the ages the mere act of *not liking them for it* is most offensive.

Yes, we love the good men in our lives and sometimes, oftentimes, the bad ones too—but that we're not in full revolution against the lot of them is pretty amazing when you consider this truth: men get to rape and kill women and still come home to a dinner cooked by one.

Somewhere along the way, I started to care more about what men thought of me than my own health and happiness because doing so was just easier. I bought into the lie that the opposite of "victim" is "strong." That pointing and laughing and making it easier on everybody was the best way to tell our stories.

But if you are sick and want to be well, you need to relay the details of your symptoms: glossing over them ensures a lifetime of illness.

My daughter is happy and brave. When she falls down or gets hurt, the first words out of her mouth are always: *I'm all right, Mom. I'm okay.* And she is. I want her to be okay always. So while my refusal to keep laughing or making you comfortable may seem like a real fucking downer, the truth is that this is what optimism looks like. Naming what is happening to us, telling the truth about it—as ugly and uncomfortable as it can be—means that we want it to change. That we know it is not inevitable.

I want the line of my mother and grandmother to stop here.

CANDY DISH

SCOOT DOWN.

The first time I had an abortion I was in this same room, on the same table. When I walked into the office, the receptionist offered me tea in the same way she had seven years earlier. I was the only patient there, an upside to paying over a thousand dollars for an early abortion in a private clinic that doesn't accept insurance: you get to be alone and hold on to a shameful sense of superiority that you aren't like other women who get later abortions.

As I lay down on the brown cushioned table, the rolled-out paper crunching beneath me, I noticed that the Jolly Ranchers on a nearby counter were in the same glass candy dish that had been there the first time I was here. Then, the candy was Starbursts.

That time I was in my late twenties. I had a job, money, and enough family support to have a baby. But I also had a shitty boyfriend, a lingering love for an even shittier ex-boyfriend, and was in the process of finishing my first book. I had always thought that should I find myself pregnant at that age, twenty-seven, I would just go through with it. But the minute I saw the word "pregnant" come up on that stick, I knew that I couldn't be.

I was only a few weeks along, but most abortions can't happen until eight or ten weeks and I couldn't wait that long. A Google search on "early abortions" that same day led me to a clinic claiming to be midwifelike that used a method for ending the pregnancy that didn't require machines, anesthesia, or a horrible sucking sound. Just a syringe and a nurse holding your hand. I made the appointment for the following week, even though the woman on the phone cautioned me not to come in too early—there would be nothing to take out if I didn't wait.

My mother had an abortion when I was nine and my sister was seven but she didn't tell me this until after I had mine. She hoped, I think, that it would be a bonding moment between us but the clear regret she had over ending her pregnancy—*Your dad was so busy with his music, I felt I had to; it's normal to feel depressed after*—made my own ambivalence feel somehow criminal.

We were sitting in a restaurant in Astoria, Queens, when she told me—a new place on 34th Avenue that had opened near the Museum of the Moving Image. The café was cavernous on the inside—literally—with high ceilings and walls made to look like bumpy stone. I know she wanted me to tell her this was the hardest thing, and to find some commonality in our suffering, but it wasn't hard and I wasn't hurting.

My parents got married when my mother was only seventeen years old, and she tells me that on their wedding night she called her mother crying afterward. She was a virgin, brought up in Catholic school, and terrified of men—even my father, whom she had dated since she was twelve years old. Her tears that night set the stage for a relationship-long narrative between them: my father desperate for her love and she too scared of it.

They were married for thirteen years before having children, my mother enduring miscarriage after miscarriage before her pregnancy with me finally took. So when she got pregnant with my sister when I was little over a year old, it was a surprise. By the time the third pregnancy came, years later, my parents were working nonstop and my father had started a blues band that was doing relatively well—several gigs a week at bars and clubs downtown, like Manny's Car Wash and the Bitter End.

When I was twelve or thirteen years old I started going to watch him play, thrilled that the bartenders would ask me for my drink order, ignoring their eye rolls when I told them my age. One night when I walked into the back room where the band was getting ready one of the men backstage made a comment about my low-slung jeans and how he could see my underwear. I became very aware, suddenly, that I was the only girl in that room and that my father wasn't there.

It never occurred to me that those late nights he was gone playing music meant my mother was alone caring for us. Or that his rehearsals several nights a week meant the same thing. It's difficult, when you are young, to imagine the time your parent spends with you as hard work.

My parents are retailers—a profession a college professor I had once called the *most evil there is* because they jack up the price of items for profit, and I thought it was pretty easy for her to say. When I was a child, they ran two stores—one in the Bronx, one in Queens—that sold women's clothing, the kind meant for older customers: bedazzled jumpsuits; nightshirts with Betty Boop cartoons on them; huge bras and underwear that only came in white, beige, and black, all stacked in yellow boxes behind the counter. Their customers yelled at them, tried to return clothing that had been worn for years, and sometimes pissed and shit themselves in the dressing room.

The store was named after my mother and the walls were slatted so that the latest shirts and elastic-waist paints could be hung there, covering the store in sets of polyester "suits" with jewelry dangling off the hanger to give a sense of a completed outfit. I liked to try on the wigs from the mannequins that were in the front windows, their outfits and surroundings changed monthly by a man who carried pins in a cushion that looked like a tomato and who once—to annoy my mother after a fight—fashioned a tuft of fake pubic hair to come out of the underwear on one of the mannequins modeling lingerie in the window.

I spent most days after school at the store in Queens—the one in the Bronx would close before I turned ten—and I would lose myself in one of two activities: (1) going to McDonald's to buy french fries so I could feed the mice that lived in the back corner of the store (my mother hated this game); (2) playing in the long satin nightgown rack.

I figured these gowns must be the most special because unlike other clothes in the store they were covered in clear plastic bags to protect them. I would pretend to dance with them: that I was a prince at a ball and these nightgowns—disembodied and smooth, covered in plastic—were princesses, and I would reach underneath the bags to feel the satin beneath. Sometimes I would stick my whole body underneath the plastic and the gown, even though my head just reached the empire waist, and my mother would yell at me to get out—that I would suffocate in there.

I learned to ask customers, *Can I help you?* as a toddler and later how to ring up a sale on an old-fashioned register where the numbers were printed on huge circular buttons that clicked in when you pressed on them, like typewriter keys. I collected hangers to put in boxes in the basement and sorted clothes by size, hanging them on the round racks in between the white S, M, L, XL, XXL, and XXXL signs that hung there too.

We didn't live far from the store, just a few avenues over in Long Island City. Our house was on the corner of a block lined with other houses but just two blocks away from rows of factories—sweatshops, my father said—and street corners that would become populated with sex workers once the sky got dark. One night when I was ten we heard a woman screaming outside for help. My father looked out the window, saw her battered face, and ran outside to her. But he, a large bushy-bearded man in his underwear, did not inspire confidence and she ran away. Hers was not the last scream we heard outside of our window.

I don't know if it was the city noise, the car alarms, or simple childhood insomnia, but I rarely slept through the night growing up. My earliest memories are of walking around our house in the darkness, trying to think of something to do to pass the time. Sometimes I would just sit at the edge of my parents' bed, hoping my presence would magically wake them up. Sometimes I pretended I was a ghost haunting my own house.

But I am older now, so when my mother tells me about her abortion, I understand logically that it must have been impossible to imagine having a baby alongside her two preteen children. Among that work, in that house, in that neighborhood they were working so hard to make sure we didn't spend too much time in.

Still, my first thought when she tells me about her abortion is one of shock because *she is such a good mother*. Always sacrificing, always putting us first. Despite my feminism and knowledge that sometimes women get abortions to be good mothers, my first thought is one of judgment.

But admitting that somewhere inside me is the belief that good mothers don't get abortions is too antithetical to the work I do and who I am, and so with loneliness masked as self-sufficiency, I made the appointment to end my pregnancy and went with my sister instead of the man who got me pregnant.

Midwifelike handholding aside, the pain was terrible, much worse than I expected. I didn't cry, but my sister told me I went pale, my lips white for the minutes afterward while I ate a pink Starburst to get my blood sugar going enough to get me off the table without vomiting.

The elevator ride down from the office was strange, being in an enclosed space with people leaving work to go out to lunch and you—in pain but trying not to show it and nauseous but trying not to throw up—just having made a decision to keep your life on track but feeling like a feminist cliché.

At least it's over, I thought. I celebrated my birthday but went for a required blood test to make sure the procedure had taken.

It had not.

As I had been warned, I tried to end the pregnancy too early. When the nurse told me on the phone my knees literally went weak at the thought of enduring that pain again. So when I went to see the doctor for the second time, I started to sob. *Please can you give me something.* She told me I was right and brave to ask for what I needed and a nurse put an IV in my arm and gave me a sedative that made the procedure so easy I cried with relief and gratitude—thanking the doctor through tears as she left the room when all was done. I left the office with my sister and went outside, where my mother was waiting with her car to drive me home, me lying down in the backseat. I knew, though, that I could never go through this again.

A few months later, I met the man who would become my husband and father of my daughter. Andrew was five years younger than I was, just out of college, and didn't wear socks—

something I chalked up as a residual idiosyncrasy from his Northern California upbringing. He had reached out to me over email, asking if I would write for the liberal website he was working with. Years later, I framed the email as a last-minute Valentine's Day gift.

We waited a few weeks before having sex, the longest I had ever waited before sleeping with a man. Most of my long-term boyfriends had morphed out of what should have been one-night stands. I told him beforehand that he should know if I ever became pregnant I wouldn't have an abortion under any circumstances. I told him what had happened months earlier and he understood.

A few months into our relationship my first book was released and his grandmother passed away. I sent flowers because it seemed like the adult thing to do and I imagined that his parents couldn't have been thrilled with their just-out-of-college son dating a woman nearing thirty. I thought that if I could prove I was a responsible kind of grown-up woman—a thoughtful person rather than the emotionally messy, desperately-searching-for-solid-ground woman-child I knew myself to be—they would like me.

Andrew went to Harvard, and before that Harvard summer schools while in high school. He was bored in his public school and had taken all the math classes they had, so they sent him to the nearby community college to study. One day at my apartment he left his computer open to a chat he was having with his last girlfriend, who was still in college. He told her what was happening between us was mostly physical, that I wasn't a real intellectual. Nine years later I never bring it up because it pains him too much to think about the young snob he was and how I must have felt, but it matched the pace for the rest of our relationship: he in love with an older woman he found exciting, me feeling distinctly unworthy.

When Andrew's parents first came to visit him in New York, he was sharing an apartment—a five-story walk-up towering over the row of Greek restaurants on 31st Avenue in Ditmars, Queens—with a guy he met on Craigslist. He was only spending one night a week there, preferring to be with me most days and to avoid a roommate who kept a three-foot cardboard cutout of himself hanging in the living room.

I lived by myself in Astoria, with new furniture I'd bought with money I got as a payoff to leave an illegal loft in Williamsburg, Brooklyn. It was the first furniture I owned that wasn't hand-me-downs from my aunts and uncles. The last couch set I'd had—a leather sectional sofa—had been given to me by a cousin who worked as a doorman at a building on the Upper East Side. The people who had owned it before were moving and didn't like it so they just left it behind and told him to take it if he wanted. He did, along with a heavy white coffee table with curved edges that alongside the black leather couch made my apartment look like a 1980s banker's place. (But ironically, because Brooklyn.)

The plan was that we would go to dinner with his parents at a nearby restaurant that had outdoor seating, but that they would come over to my apartment first for appetizers. I had pre-ordered antipasti at the local Italian deli: a block of provolone, spicy soppressata, mixed olives, pepperoncini, artichoke hearts, and salami. Andrew, irked that he would have to make a stop on the way back from work to pick up the food, didn't understand why what I had in the fridge—Ritz crackers and a block of cheddar—wouldn't do. Food is one of the few things that makes me feel comfortable and in control—I can put together a nice meal without its feeling like posturing. It's the only time I don't feel like a fraud, ironic for a professional feminist.

Before Andrew I didn't cook much for boyfriends. I had tried to make a fancy dinner for a boyfriend once, another WASP-y Harvard graduate who played piano and once fucked me in the bathroom of a New Year's Eve party even though I had just broken my finger by slamming it in the door on the way in. I made steak and fettuccine Alfredo that we ate at my parents' house, who were gone for the weekend, to avoid my then-roommate. All was going so well until while we were having sex my parents' dog farted so badly that we had to stop. When he later broke up with me, his insistence that I was the "hottest" girl he had ever dated only intensified my despair. My attempts to be the cool girl who eats giant hamburgers but loves film adaptations of Shakespeare, who interns at an international NGO but will let you fuck her through the pain of a broken finger in a dirty bathroom, failed. He knew like I knew that I belonged in only half of those situations.

It was not a coincidence that I met Andrew so soon after I ended that first pregnancy. The abortion marked the last in a succession of decisions to take hold of a life that was increasingly careening out of control. A few months before getting pregnant I had moved out of Brooklyn to stay at my parents' home in Woodstock, New York, under the auspices of writing my book.

Really, it was to avoid an ex-boyfriend whom I still loved despite all reason and proof that he had been cheating on me for the whole of our relationship, and to stop doing cocaine in earnest, breaking a nearly two-year habit that had just started to scare me. I decided, consciously, that I would not do these things anymore: drugs, date assholes, believe that my professional good fortune had nothing to do with my ability.

And so I published a book meant for young women who didn't quite know if they were feminists or not and threw a party to celebrate, and my mother brought a salad and spinach pie she made at home to put out for the people who came. Andrew was in California visiting his grandmother. And so I got drunk and snorted Adderall in the bathroom, cleaning my nostrils of the blue powder before going back out. Somehow I reasoned that it wasn't as bad as doing cocaine; also I didn't have any. Piles of the book lay on a table near the entrance to the bar, and when I thumbed to the back to see my author photo I realized that I was pregnant at the time of the picture. Smiling, unknowing, posing.

BEAUTIES

MY SISTER DIDN'T SAY A WORD ABOUT THE GASH ON HER WRIST until she was stitched up with black thread and back home. Even then, it was only to remark that the blood that had spread across her green Easter sundress looked a lot like the shape of a puppy.

She wasn't supposed to wear the dress that day—my mother was worried it would get dirty. But my sister insisted and so we walked next door, her overdressed, to play with the little girl who rented the apartment above my uncle's.

When you grow up in a family of beautiful women, the last thing you want to be told is that you look like your father. The reality was hard to miss, though. I took after my dad and my sister looked like my mother, a woman so beautiful men would politely stop her in the street to tell her so. Children did the same thing to my sister. In our neighborhood—mostly Italian, South Asian, and Brazilian at the time—she was a blond-haired, green-eyed wonder and little girls would stop her at the concrete playground sprinkler a few blocks from our house to ask to stare into her eyes.

The day she wore her good dress and her hair in pigtails, we argued with our friend about what we should play. We settled on a game called Spud, where one of us would throw a large red rubber ball into the air while the others ran down the block. Once the ball was back in your hands, you yelled out *Spud!* with the hope of catching the runners moving instead of freezing. We only played a few rounds before our neighbor accused me of cheating. I remember that I wasn't.

As she stormed up the brick stoop into the vestibule of her building, my sister followed along after her. She stood making funny faces through the glass-paned door until our neighbor finally opened it. But when she did, and saw me close behind, she slammed the door just as my sister put out her arm to stop her.

The arm shattered through one of the panes and our neighbor yelled up to her mother that we had broken it. She didn't see the blood. The red was spreading across my sister's green dress and I ran toward my house, screaming for my mother. I hopped over a metal chain-link fence to the yard shared between my aunt's house and our own. My sister walked in slowly behind me, saying nothing, blood spreading further still, pouring out of her arm onto her dress and pooling at her shoes.

My parents were in bare feet when we got into our car, a wood-paneled station wagon. My mother sat in the front seat with my sister, holding a rag onto her wrist. My father screamed *injured child injured child* out of the window, his voice a make-shift siren, as we drove to Astoria General Hospital to get the other cars out of the way when beeping wasn't working.

When we ran into the emergency room, my sister silent and

smeared with red, I remember the old women in the waiting room. One on a gurney gasped audibly at the sight of her.

Every year that went by I got more awkward while she remained beautiful—hardly sprouting a pimple except once or twice during puberty. So while she and my mother would try on clothes and earrings and makeup, I would lock myself in the upstairs bathroom to prove to myself how ugly I was by comparison. There was a large mirrored cabinet there above the sink and if I pulled all three of the doors out, I could create a three-way mirror to look at my face from all possible angles.

My nose was too big, my chin was too small. The hair on my upper lip, bleached by Jolen secretly bought at the Genovese drugstore with stashed-away lunch money, stood out against my tan skin. When you look hard enough and long enough at your own face, everything about it starts to seem hideous. Especially when you are ten.

I wrote in my diary at the time, *I'm so ugly I can't stand it. I have a big gross nose, pimples, hairy arms. I will never have a boy like me or a boyfriend. All of my friends are pretty and I will be the one with no one.*

I was feeling that loneliness acutely at the time because I was obsessed with a boy named Matt in my Roosevelt Island elementary school.* Matt—the first in a long line of blond boys I would fall for—told me once that I would be so, so pretty if not for my big nose. *He thought I could be pretty!*

---

* Some names throughout the book have been changed to protect people's privacy, in particular the names of those with whom I've had close relationships.

I loved him completely despite his short stature, bowl hair-cut, and occasional taunts. But on Halloween in the sixth grade, when he came dressed up as a baseball glove and I was a cave-woman, he said I should have won "most attractive" costume at the class contest even though a group of cruel girls asked if I was meant to be a dog since I was carrying a big plastic bone. *Most attractive!*

My parents told me later that the girls were part of a group whose parents didn't like the fact that a few kids from off of the island had been allowed into the elementary school. That we lived across a small bridge in Queens had marked us as outsiders.

Matt had a cat named Mookie and when he wasn't making fun of me he was pulling me aside to talk about the things he loved: the Mets, his mom, his cat, and maybe another cat one day. We were in every class together from the second to the sixth grade, which I took as some sort of divine intervention—proof that we were meant to be together.

I started to measure my nose. First with my fingers, which I would try to keep the same distance apart as they were when they were on my face and then bring them over to my mother and her nose to demonstrate just how much bigger mine was compared to hers. She would insist that my nose was smaller—the kind of well-meaning parenting that just inspired fury and distrust in me. The nicest thing someone said to me at that time was that a lot of people my age had big noses, and that I would eventually "grow into it." The comment acknowledged that the ugliness I was feeling was valid and not some in-my-head childish self-hatred. That comment was the only thing that gave me hope, the idea that my face would slowly morph into something more reasonable and proportional than the monstrosity I was currently working with.

Still, I started recording the size of my nose with a soft tape measure meant for hemming that my mother kept in the junk drawer. I kept the measurements in a small lavender notebook that I used to write poetry in but now wrote the numbers on the last page because I believed if my parents found it they would not think to go all the way to the back of the book.

The thing about hating your face so intently is that it takes an extraordinary amount of care and attention. The obsession is almost contradictory, because you start to love the self-hatred a little bit. It becomes a part of your routine—you whisper *I hate you* when you pass by a mirror or think the same silently when trying on clothes or putting on makeup, acts that feel foolish at the time because you know you're not tricking anyone into thinking you're beautiful. There's nothing that you could pile on your body or face that would make it worthy.

But at least I could bear to look. A friend I lived with for a short while after college had an ID card for work that she was supposed to keep hanging around her neck at all times. To avoid having to look at the picture of herself all day, she carefully cut a small piece of yellow paper into a square and taped it over her face. Later I would find plastic bags of vomit hidden underneath her bed, wrapped in towels meant to mask the smell that eventually led to their discovery.

I think a lot at the time about how my parents met in elementary school and I wonder if that means Matt and I might get married one day. I ask my parents to please let me have a nose job. Now when I look in that three-way mirror I carry a piece of paper with me that I position over the bump on my nose so I can see what I might look like if it were gone. My father tells me my nose is part of my Italian heritage, that getting rid of it would be a slap in the face to our ethnicity. I tell him we'll always have spaghetti. He is not convinced.

I imagine all of the things that would go right if I were to just have a smaller nose. I would have a boyfriend—or at the very least Matt would think about liking me back—and the girls in school would stop making fun of me. That year, several girls would bring me to a playground to have a "talk" about why we could not be friends anymore. Because I am too loud, because I agree with everything they say—desperate for approval in a way that is unseemly. *We're not trying to be mean*, they say, *it would just be better if you ate lunch somewhere else.*

I know if I looked more like them, with a small nose and long light hair in braids and bows, I would not have to travel across the island to the building where the younger children are to eat lunch with my sister.

There is only one other girl I know who travels to Roosevelt Island from Queens, a girl who moved from Costa Rica in the third grade and whom my parents give rides to since she lives only three blocks away from us. She is the cruelest one of all, throwing things in my hair as we stand in line, telling me I look like I'm wearing my clothes backward because everything I do is ridiculous. It doesn't occur to me that the piece of cardboard I saw over her window in her apartment once—she says her mom's boyfriend broke it—has been there all year.

I find out from my male friends that there are cute girls, pretty girls, hot girls, sexy girls, and sometimes variations or combinations of all of the above. The worst to be is a fat girl or an ugly girl. I was an ugly girl who became a sexy girl once my breasts grew in and I started telling dirty jokes with abandon. As soon as I "got a chest," as my mom would say, the taunts about my face stopped as boys became more interested in feeling me up than making me cry. I started to forget about my face and mean girls and focused on the things my body could do and inspire. During summer break a male friend whom I had known since childhood put his hand on my breast as we watched a movie in the room over from our parents, saying nothing. I remained frozen, unsure what to do. *Wasn't he supposed to kiss me first?* I was eleven.

Over the next few years, I become so involved in trying to forget my face that I don't notice the ways my sister is trying to disappear her body. First under long jean shorts that she wears over her bathing suit when we go to the beach in the summer. She even swims with them on, infuriating my parents, who yell at her to take them off, she looks ridiculous. A few years later the shorts are gone, along with twenty pounds. She refuses to eat anything with sugar in it, makes herself a different meal instead of eating the family dinner my mother cooks, and feels cold all of the time. My parents say she is just diet-ing, it's nothing to worry about. But a picture of her from one vacation, writing at a table, all collarbones and hollow cheeks, tells a different story. She is lucky though—she sees the same thing I do when she looks at the picture and starts eating again, just like that. She has always been stronger than most, espe-cially me.

I am only made to feel too heavy once in my life—the sum-mer after my freshman year at a college where I am introduced to drinking until you black out, "penny pitchers," and a boy who will break me. I had never stepped on a scale outside of the doctor's office until I see my grandmother during a holiday break and the first thing she says is, *Wow, you got fat.*

Years later, after I give birth to my daughter, an editor asks me to write a piece about how I lost the baby weight as I am the same number of pounds immediately after having Layla that I was the day I got pregnant. Having a two-pound baby helps, I suppose. A failing liver curbs the appetite as well. Premature birth: the hottest new diet tip for moms. Never before had being skinny felt so empty.

As people get older they get more polite, at least to your face. And so I am mostly able to forget about my nose. Or maybe I fi-nally did grow into it, I'm not sure. But I am safe from that par-ticular taunt save for some thoughtlessly cruel comments that come every few years. What helps me forget is how much these boys seem to want things from me. If they want to touch me, I think, I cannot be quite as hideous as I imagine.

When I have my first real kiss with tongue from my first real boyfriend—a friend of a friend who lives on 110th Street and Broadway—I'm waiting for the tram to Roosevelt Island on a raised platform. It feels quick and wet but I am thrilled. We speak on the phone a few more times before I ask my friend to break up with him for me; I don't remember why.

Later, I date a boy who lives in Woodstock, New York, who likes having a "city" girlfriend. He is named after a Caribbean poet, and after giving me a mix tape with "November Rain" as the first song, he put his hand under my bra while we're making out. We are in a tent that another friend put up in the backyard as part of a coed sleepover. When my parents find out there were boys with us they are not pleased but don't say much. He rubbed against me that night, rhythmically, in a way I didn't understand. He later asked me, if I didn't want to have sex, why did I let him do that?

This marks the time in my life when I first feel wanted. Not by adult strangers on the street or boys in small towns who have dated everyone they know already, but by peers. And when I start high school, seniors even. Guys, who have suddenly become so much more slick and eager, are asking me on dates to the movies or the pool hall. The second day of school my new friend James comes over to my house and my father is struck when he walks in the door by this six-foot-three-inch fourteen-year-old with green hair who may be courting his daughter.

It is not until I think carefully, weighing options I cannot believe I have, that I decide to date Jay. He still has braces and isn't as cute as some of the other guys I know but is a junior, and a graffiti artist (he says) to boot. Later, when I meet his father, he would say I have nice eyes, which I know is code for *the rest of her face is ugly*. That relationship ended with virginities lost, fights over whether or not I should be "allowed" to drink Zima, and a girl with a lip ring when he leaves for college. At the time, I was just so glad to be wanted.

Before I left Roosevelt Island to go to junior high school, I told Matt that I would be going to a different school next year—a newly opened technology-focused junior high in Manhattan. I filled out the application myself and thought I was very clever when in the box for "doodles" I drew pictures of palm trees and pyramids—a sign, I thought, they would take as an eye toward the global. *Not just any doodles!*

We talked, alone, outside of the school building standing closer than we ever had before and he promised he would come see me in the after-school plays that I performed with a local theater group. That we were friends. That it wouldn't be the last time we saw each other. But it was.

STAGES

*COME ON, HE SAYS. SHOW US HOW GOOD YOU WOULD SUCK
A DICK.*

A guy who goes to my school takes the Blow Pop lollipop
out of Jen's mouth before he puts it back in. Then he takes it out
again. At first she looks confused but when he smiles she starts
to exaggerate her lips around the red sphere and makes a coy
face. He laughs and says, *That's nice.*

We are standing in front of our junior high school building on 33rd Street, out to lunch because we're allowed to leave
school if we want to buy food at McDonald's or go to a diner
to eat.

He comes over to me next, even after I say *no way*, and grabs
the thin white lollipop stick coming out of my mouth. I clamp
my teeth down and look at him, straight in the eyes, I hope now.
He laughs again and says to his friend, *At least she wouldn't let go.*
This is how I learned what blow jobs are.

At home, I spend a few afternoons in my room with one of
my friends writing stories about sex in pen and red marker in

our white and black composition notebooks. We create dialogue and use descriptors like "hot dog" and "squirting milk." I hide the notebooks behind my dresser wrapped in a nightshirt with a kitten on the front—something my mother brought home from her store for me.

When my parents find a joking note that my friend Jen has sent me about sucking dick—about blue-purple penises and tongues—they want me not to see her anymore, insisting that anyone who writes like that knows too much. Later Jen will tell all of us that she had an abortion in the sixth grade and point to a scar on her abdomen as proof. We'll all suspect she is lying but it won't be until another friend's older sister explains how abortions are actually done that we'll know for sure. But still, we won't say anything to her.

I met my junior high school friends on the first day of school in a basement cafeteria where the overhead lights flickered. There was a group of five of them, sitting at the same table, who all lived on Governors Island because their parents were in the Coast Guard. We made the long trek to the island after school and on weekends because it's the most adult-free place I have ever been. It feels special and secret because I'm not allowed to be there unless one of my friends "sponsors" me—putting me on a list of people allowed to come on the base.

I don't think I ever meet one of my friends' parents and we spend most of our time running around playing manhunt and hanging out at the island bowling alley, which has a Burger King attached to it. Sometimes Jen pretends to get drunk on one beer.

I peed my pants! she squeals, though she hasn't. The rest of us play along though, pretending to lift her up and carry her back home.

One weekend we decide to take pictures with a disposable camera so we can enter ourselves into a *Seventeen* magazine modeling contest. We dress in what we think are our nice clothes. I wear jeans and a semisheer flowered top borrowed from a friend, and we take pictures of each other on swings, in the grass, and posed on top of rocks. When we get the pictures back, developed, we laugh at them together but secretly hope ours are maybe not so bad and maybe even the best ones and worthy of submission. One of my friends tells me if my nose *wasn't so fucking big* I would win for sure.

Another weekend we go to San Gennaro's feast downtown and buy wine coolers from a corner store that we keep in brown paper bags as we walk around. We are twelve.

We meet a group of boys who are seniors in high school and want our phone numbers even though we tell them we are in seventh grade. Instead they give us theirs, and I write the shortest one's beeper number on my arm in brown eyeliner from my purse. He tells me his uncle is John Gotti and we feign amazement. I never use his number but I also don't wash it off for a few days, hiding it from my parents under long sleeves and showing it off to my friends at school. A girl with us that night ends up getting pregnant by one of these men; I'll hear years later in high school that they maybe got married.

I don't tell my friends that one day a week after school I am going to acting class, putting on year-end plays like I have every year since second grade. It seems too eager, too uncool.

I STARTED PERFORMING IN THE THIRD GRADE, A YEAR AFTER MY parents got me into an elementary school on Roosevelt Island—the result of a months-long campaign to have my sister and me transferred out of our shitty zoned school in Queens. The first play we put on was *Oliver*, and I was cast as both an orphan and "Old Sally," a character who gives someone a locket at some point. I don't remember why.

In the first of three performances, when I got out onstage for my Old Sally lines I realized that I had left the locket on the prop table, where it was outlined with a black marker. And so instead of saying my lines, I stayed mute and didn't move, didn't breathe, while the audience laughed. After the laughing died down and it was silent again, a fellow cast member ran offstage to get the locket and came back to bring it to me. Only when the necklace was in my hands, my fingers wrapped around the locket, was I able to speak again.

I started to get better parts and more lines, which I traced over with yellow highlighter to help me memorize them. By sixth grade I landed a lead: Rosie in *Bye Bye Birdie*. I was the youngest girl to get the role, and I was supposed to feign sexiness and experience. My big solo required me to rip off a jacket to reveal a fringed and red-sequined short skirt underneath. I got to wear bright pink lipstick. The choreographer—one of my friends' mom—whispered in my ear before I went onstage that I should *bring it hard.*

Later, I played Nancy in *Little Mary Sunshine*—a character who has a boyfriend but loves attention from any and all men. One of my songs is "Naughty Nancy," and in another I sang about wanting to be like a spy who seduces men for information. *Oh what a wicked girl was she, that's the kind of girl I want to be.*

My friend Dave, who was in the theater group with me, said I probably got the part because I had the "figure" for it. Even at eleven years old Dave talked like he was a grown man. A few years later he would ask me if I knew my boyfriend "in the biblical sense." *You mean like fucking?*

I continued to perform throughout high school, and we did fewer musicals in favor of "real" plays. The better parts started to go to kids whose parents gave the most money to the theater, we heard, and my parents gave nothing. On the last day of our last performance the woman who had taught and directed me from third grade on, who had the same name as my mother, gave me a card saying she was proud of me, listing off some of the roles I'd had over the years. Later, after the show, I compared mine with that of another friend who was also a senior. Except for the list of roles, the inscription in her card said the same thing that mine did word for word. A few other people, those who played more main characters, got messages that were longer, more personalized.

MY DAUGHTER IS NERVOUS. SHE'S FIVE YEARS OLD, BUT SHE knows that once she turns six, she'll have to dance on a real stage in front of a real audience for her ballet performance. Right now, at the end of the year, parents take off their shoes and file into a small ballet studio and sit in folding chairs up against the mirrored wall and watch their children perform in the same room that they learn in weekly. We watch these tiny humans dance and jump around with complete abandon and joy. They wave to us, trip and fall, their headbands falling down around their eyes, and they don't care because their parents and grandparents are right there smiling and taking pictures.

But when they turn six, the performance moves to a stage—a fact that both thrills and terrifies Layla. She wants to be a "real ballerina" but is afraid of all the people watching her. I tell her not to worry because the people in the audience are on her side. They will be thrilled just to see her dance happily.

She wants to know if her teacher can come up with her, if she can wait in the wings or just dance like she normally does— for her parents, in a room with her friends. The night before her last performance as a five-year-old child I have a dream about being in a play that I never bothered to learn the lines for. A dream about yellow highlighters and scripts bound in three-ring binders that I desperately thumb through in the moments before I'm supposed to step onstage.

I want to tell her that she can quit, that she doesn't need to perform if she doesn't want to. But I know it's bad advice, setting a bad example. I also know that she might like being onstage. Sometimes the best moments are right before a performance when you're backstage putting on makeup that you would normally never wear and fixing your hair in a certain way and looking at the lineup of costumes you'll have on. And then when it's done, when you get onstage, the hot lights make you sweat but the way people look at you, look to you, for how they should feel and what to do is a power of sorts. I have always liked it, despite the fear.

MEASUREMENTS

I WAS WALKING FROM THE CITY HALL SUBWAY STATION TO MY high school on Chambers Street when I noticed my nipples sticking out. The white shirt with the small bow on the neckline had seemed sweet when I put it on that morning, but outside of the darkened train tunnels I could see the outline of my areolas when I looked down.

I had neglected to wear a "T-shirt bra"—the slightly padded lie that female breasts are Barbie-smooth. I crossed my arms in front of my chest but soon realized that would be an impossible pose to keep throughout the day in class and in the hallways. So I pulled the straps of my JanSport backpack a few inches off my shoulders and in, so that their shadow would cover the points. It started to rain.

I have normally had very good luck with my breasts. They grew at a reasonable pace, at a normal age, and by the time I was twelve or thirteen years old I wore a respectable B cup. The real fortune, though, was that before then—when I needed my first bra—I didn't have to go far to get it. My parents' lingerie and clothing store, though hopelessly uncool, was an easy place to get a training (AAA-cup) bra without the embarrassment of department store shopping. For some girls this was a rite of passage with their mothers; for me it was just another day at my mom's store—with my aunt, who was the manager—watching on.

A salesgirl (she was in her sixties, but this is what they were called) named Mickey helped to measure me, taking me into the small dark dressing room with an accordion-style door and pressing limp white tape up against my skin. Looking back, I realize this must have been just for show because I had no real breasts to speak of yet, but I appreciated the formality with which she measured me. I got three bras: one in white, one in beige, and one in black. They were ribbed cotton and had a bow in the middle where my cleavage should have been.

Within two years, I was wearing a full C cup. So at fourteen years old, I had the body that I would always have. Outside of the leers from strange men on the subway, though, I didn't give a lot of thought to my breasts. I was glad to have them, glad that I was "normal." Glad that I had something, finally, that made me forget about my face. And so when I left junior high with what I thought seemed like a reasonably womanish body and improving makeup skills, I was optimistic that I could leave behind my reputation as the nerdy one of my friends.

Stuyvesant High School was supposed to be the best public high school in the city. Or at least the hardest to get into. We were a school of consummate test-takers, students who were praised simply for our presence at a freshman orientation in a packed Tribeca auditorium where we were told by the principal that "cream rises to the top." To get into the school students had to take an SAT-like test that would qualify them for admission, hopefully, to one of three specialized schools in New York. Those with the highest grades went to Stuy.

My parents started talking to me about this test when I was still in elementary school. *You're going to Stuyvesant, right, Jessica?* my dad would ask in front of my aunts, uncles, and sometimes strangers in bookstores or parks. My father—so smart as a boy that he skipped seventh grade—had wanted to go to the school. But at thirteen years old he got caught stealing a car and a guidance counselor told him he was no longer eligible to take the entry test. This was a lie that shaped the rest of his young adulthood, a missed opportunity that I was expected to make up for.

I was to take the test for the same reason my parents spent months working the education system to move us to the elementary school on Roosevelt Island, sent me to a ballet class that I hated and was too clumsy for, and later would make me visit colleges that I had no chance of getting into. It was a move that a friend from the Bronx would later call the "outer-borough shuffle"—the hustle of middle-class parents who had the time and knowledge to fuck with the system. A lot of times it worked, a lot of times it didn't. But either way it left me with the feeling that I should always try for more than I had been given, even if I felt unsure what to do once I got it.

And so my father and my mother put money aside and sent me to a Kaplan course every week for months before the test was scheduled. I rode the subway to a midtown classroom where I would take practice tests and learn how to strategically skip questions, narrow down answers, and otherwise up my chances of getting in. My parents tell me that I didn't sleep for weeks before the test, instead walking around the house in the middle of the night. The evening after I finally completed the test, though—sitting in a room in the old Stuyvesant building in the East Village surrounded by strangers and a few friends from junior high—I slept for thirteen hours straight. My parents tell me this is how they knew that I got in.

In a school of math and science aficionados, the girl with well-developed boobs is queen. I went from being the dowdy friend of cute girls to the dowdy friend with big tits. I was being asked on dates, a lot of dates. Proper dates to pool halls and movie theaters, lunches at a diner on the weekend or a walk to Central Park. I had boyfriends—more than one! Later, in between high school relationships, my male friends would jokingly/not jokingly ask to "talk business" with me—code for *let's negotiate how it's in your best interest to suck my dick*. I turned them down but was secretly pleased nonetheless. It hadn't yet occurred to me that the boys my age would want to hook up for any other reason than *they liked me*.

I was not the smartest kid in the class anymore. To my friends and the high-achieving types around me, I was barely literate. That I could cut class and still come out with a good grade irked them. That I didn't mind when I got a shitty grade baffled them. Instead I was the girl who lost her virginity freshman year, who wore tight tops and bright lipstick. The girl who embarrassed her best friends by talking too much and too loudly about sex and joked about penis sizes. The girl who, when given an assignment to come up with the first line of dialogue in a play written in iambic pentameter, handed in a page of paper that read, "So how / long did / it take / for him / to come."

I got 95s in the classes I loved and 65s in the classes I hated, making me what the guidance counselors there would consider low achieving, an embarrassment to a school full of Westinghouse science award winners and National Merit Scholars. Students with just-okay grades were roundly ignored in favor of the real students, the ones who could up the school's rate of kids who got into Ivies. My counselor/gym teacher had one meeting with me, recommended I go to a city community college, and never spoke to me again.

I tried not to think about it and ended my senior year with a trip to the Bahamas—a weeklong vacation not sanctioned by the school but put together by student "leaders" who made it sound official enough that our parents thought it safe to ship off their teens to the beach during spring break. We were seventeen and eighteen years old but still were able to get free amaretto sours in the hotel casino and then, later, take buses to a club where we had to wear bracelets marking us as underage. They served us anyway.

The first night that my friends and I tried the green "hand

grenade" cocktails served in plastic cups with huge straws, we decided to enter a wet T-shirt contest. We lined up near the stage, giggling, believing someone would throw a bucket of water on us as we wore white shirts emblazoned with the club's logo. When we got onstage, though, the three of us watched as other girls—college girls and adult women—started to take their clothes off. All of their clothes. The music was too loud to hear if they said anything as they did this, and the men's screams from the audience almost drowned out the music anyway. The more the women danced, the closer the audience inched to the stage, some hands grabbing at their ankles as they walked by. There was no water.

We whispered to each other on the staircase leading to the stage, asking what we were supposed to do when our turn came around. The bouncer behind us had our real shirts in a pile in his arms. We finally settled on a quick flash and laughed as we did it, and hurried offstage.

Later, on the dance floor, a short man in his fifties walked up to me, smiling, and leaned in close. *I thought you should have won,* he said. I said thank you.

During that trip I found out that a boy named Joe liked me, and because he had gotten good-looking over the course of the year I hooked up with him on the dance floor of a club and then later, in his hotel room. The hand job I was giving him was taking too long, though, so I blew him instead to get it over with. I didn't think much of him the rest of the trip until at the airport waiting to go home he yelled at me in front of a crowd that you can't just suck someone's dick and then leave. I was hungover and apologized a few weeks later. For what, I wasn't sure. I just felt confused as to why he cared so much.

Before we graduated my male friends—a group of guys whom I loved and revered as hilarious and down-to-earth—let it slip that they had a nickname for me: *Valentitty*. I laughed when they told me this because that is what you do when you want to be the cool-girl friend who doesn't give a shit. The girl who isn't uptight like the others.

JESSICA VALENTI BREAST.

If you Googled my name in 2006, this was one of the first "related searches" that came up as a suggestion.

If you're searching for Jessica Valenti, maybe you're also looking for her tits!

This algorithmic embarrassment was the result of a twenty-second-long interaction in which I took a group photo with President Bill Clinton along with other then-bloggers. Soon after, a law professor/blogger posted the picture online and suggested I was posing provocatively, that I had worn inappropriate clothing, and that I "should have worn a beret."

"Blue dress would have been good too," she wrote.

This woman, known in part for her rants on YouTube, encouraged her followers when they published suggestive comments. One wrote a limerick about my fellating the former president. Another suggested I was too plain to inspire the Monica comparisons. I got phone calls with men breathing and laughing.

Soon, hundreds of blogs were dissecting what I thought was a perfectly innocuous picture, debating whether my posture suggested I was trying to stick my tits out, whether I had worn a tight sweater on purpose—one podcast even theorized that as I wasn't nearly important enough to be invited to such a meeting I must have been placed there to entice Clinton into an affair.

The mainstream media picked it up. The political video show *Bloggingheads*—which would later be run at the *New York Times*—devoted an episode to it, with the founder of the series, Bob Wright, calling me the "famous breast woman." A young reporter at Politico also covered the story, inviting the beforementioned law professor to expound on the months-long harassment campaign, which he called a "dust-up."

Jessica Valenti, who runs and blogs on feministing.com, is standing at an angle with a slight arch in her back, making the focal point of the photo, whether intentional or not, her breasts. Valenti isn't shy about her body; she just published a book called Full Frontal Feminism: A Young Woman's Guide to Why Feminism Matters.

Publishing a book with a catchy title meant I *wasn't shy about my body*. When I called him on the carpet (Feministing post title: "Two Words for POLITICO: Fuck. You."), the reporter and Politico doubled down, publishing a live chat on the topic. One reader asked why he didn't talk to me before publishing the story.

My research consisted of reading Althouse and Valenti's version of what happened, and speaking with Althouse. I e-mailed Valenti to speak with her about it but she says that she didn't get it. I can't find it in my sent mail so something must have malfunctioned.

"Malfunctioned."

We can also wade into the dispute between Althouse and Valenti: Does Valenti use sexuality for self-promotion? If she does, who cares? And if she does and nobody cares, why not just say so?

I am just grateful memes weren't too big a thing yet. Here is the truth: I look good in that photo. My breasts are fine. But I cannot help their presence in a picture that I also inhabit. I cannot help what or that you think about them.

As I read through comment after comment, blog post after blog post, I cried in the living room of my parents' house. My mother, who has always lived in Queens and rarely has left, said she was considering looking this blogger up, taking a plane to Wisconsin, and kicking her ass. My mother does not make idle threats: my father later told me she had researched flights.

Weeks earlier, when I told my parents I had been invited to meet President Clinton, they had both started weeping. They told family, friends, and random people who came into their store. Before the group picture became a joke about blow jobs and interns, they had it tacked up behind their cash register.

I was proud, too, but said nothing at the actual meeting— too afraid of sounding stupid. I was the youngest person in the room and knew I didn't deserve to be there. The "dustup" around the photo just confirmed it.

Right before I started blogging, I went to my five-year high school reunion. I was excited to drive home this point to friends I hadn't seen since graduation, friends to whom I was "a character" and the "fun" one.

While on line to get into the party, I ran into someone who was a friend on the periphery of our group—a tall nice guy who none of us knew was insanely wealthy until his mom threw him a surprise graduation party at their Brooklyn Heights duplex. We tried to catch up as we moved forward, closer to the party. He told me about Harvard and when I mentioned to him I was in graduate school he laughed. *That's the last thing I expected to hear about you*, he said. I got drunk and took him home.

SUBWAYS

THE TWO WORST TIMES FOR DICKS ON SUBWAYS: WHEN THE train car is empty or when it's crowded. As a teenager, if I found myself in an empty car, I would immediately leave—even if it meant changing cars as the train moved, which terrified me. Because if I didn't, I just knew the guy sitting across from me would inevitably lift his newspaper to reveal a semihard cock, and even if he wasn't planning on it I sure wasn't going to sit there and worry about it for the whole ride.

On crowded train cars I didn't see dicks; I felt them. Pressing into my hip, men pretending that the rocking up against me was just because of the jostling of the train—but you know differently because the rhythm is all wrong.

On the worst day, in eighth grade, I didn't notice at all. The train was crowded but my mind was elsewhere. I was listening to A Tribe Called Quest on my Walkman and thinking about how warm it was and when I stepped out of the subway onto the 39th Avenue platform the sun hit my face and I was happy to be almost home. But when I started to put my hand in my back pocket, I felt something wet: I had made it the whole ride back without noticing that a man, whose face I would never see, had come on me. I wiped my hand on the lower leg of my jeans and looked around to see if anyone had noticed. I walked the three blocks home with my backpack slung as low as possible so that no one walking behind me could see what had happened or would think I peed on myself.

I peeled the jeans off when I got home and even though most of the semen had landed on the pocket of the pants—giving me two, rather than just one, layers of protection—the skin on my ass was still damp from it. I ran the tub until there were two inches of scalding water along the bottom, squirted in some of my sister's Victoria's Secret vanilla-scented bath gel, and sat in it quickly, my shirt still on.

I wrapped a pink towel around myself when I stepped out of the tub and turned my jeans inside out before putting them in the laundry basket so my mother wouldn't find out. I knew she would cry. I knew her worst nightmare was something happening to me that in any way resembled the things that had happened to her. I piled some sheets on top of the jeans to be safe.

Later I would find out that the guy rubbing up on you in the subway isn't just an asshole—he has a disorder, with a name that sounds more like fancy cheese than a word that means "bouncing into you on the N train until he jizzes on your pants."

In the *Diagnostic and Statistical Manual of Mental Disorders*, the American Psychiatric Association describes "frotteurism" as "recurrent, intense, or arousing sexual urges or fantasies, that

involve touching and rubbing against a non-consenting person."
There are online forums for men—because, let's be real, frot-
teurs are almost exclusively men—who rub on women and girls
on the train, in bars, wherever they can do it while getting off
unnoticed.

They have handles like "Bum Feeler" and "Rock Hard"
and share stories of their exploits and pictures of the women
they have surreptitiously dry-humped. Some give advice—like
backing away occasionally so your victim gets the impression
that you're working hard not to touch her and that any contact
is the fault of the crowd.

"Women are forgiving if you can make it seem like this,"
writes Rock Hard. "Almost like you can't help it, not like you've
preyed on them like a piece of meat."

I USED TO JOKE WITH MY HIGH SCHOOL GIRLFRIENDS THAT I
must have some sign on my head only visible to men that flashes
Yes, sir, I would LOVE to see your penis! The first time I ever saw
one was on the platform for the N train three blocks away from
my house, at the 39th Avenue station.

I had just missed a train on my way to junior high, so I was
the only person there other than a man all the way at the other
end of the platform. He was so far away that I only saw the outline of his shape, but soon I noticed his hand moving furiously—
and that he was walking quickly toward me with his penis in his
hand. I had always thought myself prepared for something like

this; I knew I was supposed to yell or run, but I just stood there. I didn't look away or turn around, and even though I felt my knees giving out, my feet felt strongly planted to the ground.

As another train started to pull into the station, he stopped midway down the platform and zipped himself up. The doors of the train opened and he walked on, normally. My feet still in the same place, I tapped a man in a suit coming off the car on the shoulder and asked for help in a small voice but he didn't stop moving. So I stood there. When the next train came, I got on, figuring I should get to school—but got off one stop later at Queens Plaza to call my parents from a station phone booth when I noticed that my hands and face had pins and needles from my breathing strangely.

Every day after that, my father walked me up the stairs to the platform to wait for the train with me. The booth worker let him through the gate without paying after my dad explained to him what had happened. He gave him a bag of cherries from the tree that grew in our yard as a thank-you every week, for months.

As we were talking on the platform under the sun, I noticed an odd shape under my father's jacket. He tried to distract me with a joke but when I asked him about it a second time he pulled up his shirt to show me the metal pipe that was sticking out the top of his pants. He assured me that no cop would ever arrest him for beating a man who flashes children. Today he tells me he knows that was a lie, but he brought the pipe with him anyway.

I invested in a pair of headphones so I wouldn't have to listen to the things that men say to twelve-year-old girls on the subway. But only being able to see the looks they gave me and the way they mouthed the words made the silent come-ons seem threatening in a way they hadn't before. One man in a business suit—whose manicured nails I had noticed as he held the subway bar—lifted my headphone off one ear, came close enough that I felt his breath on my ear, and softly said, *Take care of your titties for me.* He stepped off the train as the headphone snapped back onto my head.

I started seeing dicks so regularly on my school commute—behind newspapers, barely tucked into unzipped jeans, or with just the head peeking out of sweatpants waistbands—I started to assume every man on the subway was thinking about showing me his penis. Any time the man sitting next to me brushed his hands near his pants, I stiffened—ready to get up and move seats or yell at him if I was in that kind of mood. To this day, if I'm on a plane or train, or even in a cab, if a man rests his hands on his lap I become hyperaware, waiting.

When I visited other small cities, or went upstate to Woodstock, I was shocked at how little it happened. No one yelled from their car or walked up close behind me on the street. It felt so silent and strange.

The older I got, the less it happened. By the time I was eighteen years old, I would only be flashed on the subway once or twice a year. That summer, between my freshman and sophomore years of college, I got an internship at a film magazine in

Manhattan thanks to a friend of my uncle's who was working at *George*. I went to Macy's with my mother to pick out a royal-blue pair of pants and a printed, coordinating blue shirt.

On the first morning of the job, I walked the usual blocks down to the station wearing my new outfit and a pair of low black pumps that gave me blisters. I was a few feet from the staircase leading up to the train platform when a car pulled over and a man shouted out from his opened window, asking if I knew where Northern Boulevard was. I pointed toward it—two blocks ahead—hardly glancing over, trying not to break my stride. *I'm sorry*, he said. *I don't understand. Where is it?*

I stepped off the curb to get closer to his car. Before I could point again to where he needed to go, I saw that his penis was out and that he was not really rubbing it like most men did, but shaking it. I was annoyed and tried to turn on my right heel to step back onto the sidewalk. But this man in the car grabbed me by my elbow and started pulling me toward the window. His left hand moved up to grab my shoulder, close to my neck, while he still shook his limpish dick with his right hand. He tried to pull me in further, and now my whole arm and shoulder were through his window and in the car. I pushed him on top of the head with my free hand and he let go.

My parents were at work, so instead of going to my internship I walked to my aunt's house next door, where she promptly gave me a shot of bourbon, *to calm you*, she said. I cried that I was stupid to step off the curb and she said, *Yes you were*. My cousin, who was visiting her, said, *Ma, don't make her feel worse*, but she said now I would remember next time never to do that again. And I did.

The police came, and I rode in the back of the cruiser to help look for his car—a silly exercise in futility that in retrospect I'm sure was to just make me feel better and them feel useful. But I didn't remember if the car the man was in had two doors or four, if it was white or cream. I told them I thought he made a left underneath the train (they're elevated in Queens) but they pointed out that you could only make rights. I was afraid that they would smell the bourbon on my breath and think I was a drunk teen who made it up since I couldn't remember anything, but they wrote things down and gave me an address to go to when I had the time.

I spoke to a detective at the police station a few days later; he called the man in the car a "potato head" and put me at a table with five huge books of mug shots. The label on the books said HISPANIC even though I told them I couldn't be sure of his race.

When I asked if they could give me fewer books, I was told that these were all the photos of Hispanic men in our precinct who had been arrested for sex-related crimes. Five books. They were heavy.

I didn't recognize anyone but spent several hours leafing through the books, touching the photos of the men within blocks of me who had been arrested for sex crimes. Young men, old men, very old men. When I asked the detective if they thought they would find the man who grabbed me, he looked at me across his dirty desk and shook his head. *No, sweetheart, we'll never find him.*

THERE IS A LOOK THAT COMES OVER MEN'S FACES RIGHT BEFORE they are about to say something horrible to you.

Or make a noise at you, or whistle in your general direction.

By the time I was fourteen years old I could spot this look a half a block away. In the same way I can tell if someone is a tourist by their shoes or if a person has recently done heroin, I can predict that a man is going to be an asshole on the street—sort of like a depressing New York City sixth sense.

And the moment when you take those few steps before crossing paths with the man who you know is about to say or do something is the moment when you look down, or turn your head to face across the street, or put your earphones in—as if to signal that you won't see them no matter what they do. That they are invisible to you.

Of course, they do it anyway. And you see it, or hear it.

Sometimes it's not as bad as you thought, it's a *Hey, beautiful* or a simple hello. But more often than not it's a lascivious intake of breath or a clicking noise, or sometimes just a smirk while they stare at your breasts as you walk by. Once it was a man who came close to my ear and said, *I want to eat you.* No matter the content, the message is clear: we are here for their enjoyment and little else. We have to walk through the rest of our day knowing that our discomfort gave someone a hard-on.

We're trapped in between huge bodies unable to move, too afraid to yell or bring attention to ourselves. We are trapped on the train, in the crowd, in the street, in the classroom. If we have no place to go where we can escape that reaction to our bodies, where is it that we're *not* forced? The idea that these crimes are escapable is the blind optimism of men who don't understand what it means to live in a body that attracts a particular kind of attention with magnetic force. What it feels like to see a stranger smiling while rubbing himself or know that this is the price of doing business while female. That public spaces are not really public for you, but a series of surprise private moments that you can't prevent or erase.

And so you put your headphones on and look straight ahead and don't smile even when they tell you to and just keep walking.

1995

IN MY JUNIOR YEAR OF HIGH SCHOOL, I HAD CUT ONE OF MY classes for weeks. But my teacher said he could still pass me. All I had to do was give him a hug.

At first I was thrilled to be in a class with a teacher that I'll call Mr. Z. He was a well-known easy grader and kind of a joke in a sad-old-man way; he had what we suspected was a glass eye, a hard time keeping drool in his mouth as he spoke, and walked with difficulty. The kind of classes he taught were normally held on the sixth floor, but administrators made sure he was out of sight on the tenth.

On the first day of class, Mr. Z told us that if anyone came in to observe the class—"an important-looking person"—we should raise our hand no matter what question he asked.

If you don't know the answer, raise your right hand. If you do know the answer, raise your left. I'll only call on you if you're raising the left!

Everyone looked around at each other, smirking. The social currency at Stuyvesant High School wasn't coolness as much as it was ambition and the ability to get good grades, even if you didn't deserve them—and easy teachers were a necessity for students who had overloaded on calculus and AP science classes. (I was not one of those students.)

Mr. Z didn't really teach as much as he showed movies like *Braveheart*, but one day he had an actual lesson. And though he almost never called on students, he called on me. *Come up to the board, Jessica.* He smiled, small bits of white spit accumulating at the corners of his mouth. *We all want to get a closer look at your shirt.*

He laughed, but the class was silent. I wasn't really wearing a shirt but a brown bodysuit, which was popular at the time—it snapped at the crotch and I wore it with jeans baggy enough to see the cutout above my hips. I remember the way I slid sideways through rows of desks, my arms crossed over my chest. I don't remember what I wrote on the board. I never went back to the class.

When I started at Stuyvesant as a freshman, I went from being one of the smartest kids in my junior high school to being a nominally good student without the same drive and pedigree of my cute and smart girlfriends. Their parents had gone to college, grad school even. They lived on the Upper West Side or in Park Slope in apartments filled with books and paintings and cabinets full of alcohol. One friend had an entire floor of a four-story park-side brownstone as their "room." I lived in a house where once or twice a week my mom would go outside wearing yellow rubber gloves to clean up the used condoms that littered the sidewalk from the men who parked there with prostitutes.

One of my best girlfriends was a lithe dancer who had professional head shots for when she did the occasional acting job. She was the kind of WASP-y pretty I desperately wanted to be—the type of beauty that provoked starry-eyed crushes instead of ass slaps. She lived in a duplex apartment with a spiral staircase, and we bonded as freshmen over our junior-year boyfriends. The first time she came over to my house, she remarked how much she liked my mom's "uneducated" accent. *It's cute!* she said, smiling as she helped herself to a soda from the fridge.

That same year I was called to the board in Mr. Z's class, 1995, Stuyvesant started investigating an English teacher for describing sex fantasies and his masturbation routine during class. He talked about having a dream in which he raped a maid who had his wife's face. Another student said he asked her to play Spin the Bottle with him and later let her out of writing an essay because she was "pretty." He was suspended for a few months, and then four years later—after a different man, an assistant principal, was arrested for fondling and exposing himself to a freshman—he was suspended again. That first time, though, the feigned outrage in the school only lasted as long as the newspaper articles did. We had a brief student assembly on the subject and moved on.

My favorite French teacher also had complaints filed against him. But he was dapper and wore suits to class and asked me and my friends what kind of wine we liked. So while we weren't clear on the details of the accusations against him, my friends and I felt quite strongly at the time that they were total bullshit. He didn't *need* to harass anyone.

One day, as this teacher walked alongside me and one of my friends on Chambers Street, he told us about the girl—this troubled girl, he called her—who had made up lies about him.

I was trying to help her, to tutor her! he said. *But because she knew she would fail the class anyway, this is what she said. She is very troubled.*

I felt older and important that he was confiding in us, and it never occurred to me that perhaps a teacher should not be discussing the sexual harassment allegations against him with a sixteen-year-old student. That this in itself was a violation of boundaries escaped me. Because we were *so smart*. So we just nodded our heads in agreement.

Yes, she was clearly very troubled.

STUYVESANT'S BUILDING IN TRIBECA WAS BRAND-NEW WHEN I started high school—ten floors of never-before-used hallways and lockers, classrooms and labs. We walked across a bridge that hung over the West Side Highway to get into the building, on the second floor. Everything was pristine but the escalators were always breaking.

There was a hallway on the third floor of my school where friends and I would meet when cutting class. Chris was probably the only other student there as much as I was. He kept a pillow in his locker and lay out on the floor, his baggy jeans riding up at the ankle to show off neon socks. He rode a skateboard and carried around a boom box and had huge blue eyes. We joked that we were Cliff and Norm, the regulars.

One night at a friend's house party in Brooklyn I watched from an upstairs window as my friend—yet another dancer—performed ballet moves on the sidewalk and Chris helped her, holding her hand. I tried to find a place to sleep, wandering from one room to the next, but none were empty. So I drank a forty-ounce of Olde English and agreed to go to the basement with a short blond guy named Mick. We were both wearing V-neck white shirts. The basement floor was cold, and Mick kept trying to put his hands down my pants. *You don't even like me,* I told him. He assured me I was "mad cool."

Mick kept pressing my breasts together with his hands, which I thought was strange but would make for a good story for my friends later. It took a few times of his doing this, then his putting my hands on my own breasts, before I realized he wanted to put his dick in between my breasts as I held them to-gether. I laughed at him. *Are you fucking serious?* I asked. I gave him a hand job instead.

As he was finishing he picked up a white shirt off the floor, came in it, and handed it to me.

Sorry, I said. *That was your shirt.* A look of disgust came over his face as I picked up my clean V-neck and walked up the stairs. Later that night he hooked up with our host's younger sister's friend. My friends and I laughed about how he was able to pull it off while wearing a shirt covered in his own jizz.

A few months later, after Chris and my dancer friend broke up, I hooked up with him during a party at my house. The light was starting to shine through the windows and almost everyone was asleep or trying to be. We were lying next to each other, in a room where there were five or ten other people sleeping. We made out and I gave him a hand job—surprised to find he was uncircumcised—and wrote in my diary the morning after: "I am the woman. I am so fucking fly."

He went on to date someone else, breaking my heart, but a few years later I slept with him and continued to sleep with him on and off for a few years whenever the two of us were between relationships or sometimes even if we weren't. I would hang out and watch him DJ at a terrible bar that let underage drinkers in with abandon until he was done, when the bar closed, and would drive back to his basement apartment in Brooklyn to have sex. He told me he thought about fucking me doggy style when he masturbated and one morning when he drove me home to Queens he stuck his hand down my pants and put a finger inside—*I want to think about you being wet on the way back home*—so it's hard to be too sad about how that one ended up.

THERE WERE ALWAYS RUMORS IN OUR HIGH SCHOOL ABOUT AN apartment that three teachers owned together near the school where they would take turns bringing students, but no one really knew if it was true. And even if it was, we didn't care because we thought we were so fucking cosmopolitan that the idea of teachers conspiring to molest students didn't strike us as criminal, just pathetic and disgusting. So much so that it became a joke among my friends how a teacher who had known me since I was thirteen years old—a man in his thirties—called my parents' home in Woodstock and asked me to "hang out" a few days after I graduated. I was seventeen years old at the time. He referred to himself by his first name, which I didn't really know, so it took me a few minutes to realize that the man asking if I wanted to see a movie was the same man who had taught me for years. I don't remember what I said to him in return, just that it was some version of no.

It never occurred to me that school should be a sanctuary from the bullshit that was happening outside, the catcalls and subway flashers, the gropers and perverts. This was just what men were like. This was just what being a girl was.

A few weeks before my first semester of junior year was going to end, I ran into Mr. Z in the hallway, and he pointed at me, smiling. He was wearing a striped shirt that was slightly discolored in spots, and his belly was hanging low over his pants. *I've been missing you!* he said as he walked up to me. He was breathing heavily, as if the walk down the hall had taken effort. He asked if I still wanted a good grade. I responded that of course I did.

Just give me a hug, then, he said, opening his arms. *All I want is a hug from you.*

I aced the class.

PART II

I pray you, do not fall in love with me,

For I am falser than vows made in wine.

—Rosalind, *As You Like It*, William Shakespeare

THE YARD

MY FATHER HAS A STORY THAT HE LIKES TO TELL ABOUT THE TIME he died. He was working at his father's laundromat—one of a few small businesses my grandfather opened over the years—when he fell into a vat of cleaning fluids and the fumes overcame him. But before he knew it, he was unconscious and saw a tunnel and light ahead of him. It only stopped, he says, when my grandfather saw him there and pulled him by the back of his shirt out of the container. He says it felt like he was traveling backward until his eyes opened.

My dad's name is Phil but when he's in Woodstock, New York—where he and my mother built a house from the foundation up, just the two of them—he goes by Philie. *Philie Lama* we call him, the Italian-American Buddhist who goes to meditation workshops but might blow up if you ask him to lower the music or go to a different restaurant than the one he likes.

My parents have always left out a lot when they speak about their childhood, but the violence comes out in dribs and drabs. Rumors of my father throwing a man through the window of a bowling alley for beating up his younger brother. Of my mother hiding from her drunk father and handsy uncles. Of shoplifting (my mom) and of being beaten near to death by a group of boys from a rival neighborhood (my dad). Of why you shouldn't trust cops. My cousin told me once about my father catching a thief in our house and chasing him down the block with a hammer. I don't know if he caught him or, if he did, what happened next.

My parents married when my mother was seventeen because they were in love but also to get away from their families, who had disappointed them in ways big and small from the time they were young. They moved across the country from Queens to Washington in 1966—taking a bus the whole way—so my father could look for work at a Boeing factory. They didn't stay for long.

My aunt, my father's sister, was married and had four children by the time she was twenty-one years old with a man who was taking too many drugs and seemed to be suffering from a mental illness to boot. He was my father's friend. He sounded bad on the phone, my father said, and so they came home to visit and check on him. When my dad walked into the house, one of the children had an odd look on his face and said something about Daddy being in the basement. When my father walked down the stairs, he found his friend, his brother-in-law, hanging there. He doesn't talk about what he looked like.

And so he and my mother stayed in Queens, to help with the children, who were all under seven years old at the time.

They stayed even as my cousins grew up and my family started to move to Westchester to get out of the neighborhood. Instead of leaving the city, my parents bought the foundation of a house in Woodstock, in upstate New York, from a man who couldn't continue building it. He had broken his back trying to take down one of the barns on the property; there were two of them, both over a hundred years old. The man made the mistake of disassembling the structure while still inside. It crashed down around and on top of him and so he sold the house as it was, with a set of blueprints that my parents spread out often on our table in Queens.

We started driving up every weekend, every summer, for years until my parents finished building their house. My father did the plumbing, my mom the wiring. They had a friend, an artist, collect rocks from Esopus Creek nearby and build a beautiful if a bit off-kilter fireplace. My sister and I would pee outside, help to carry the wood planks for the upstairs floor, and climb up a ladder—before we had a staircase—to our bedrooms, which were right next to each other.

After a few summers it was done, but thirty years later you can still see the remnants of my parents' mistakes. The light switches are a bit too low and in strange places. You get hot water by turning the spigot to the right, not the left. Sound carries everywhere. There is no room where your voice won't be heard.

My father wanted desperately for me to succeed and I wanted desperately to please him, to be the shining example, the proof, of how far he had come. When I did something right, something good and smart and worthy, his praise was effusive, all-encompassing. Mistakes, though, were never simply screwups. Any failure was a sure sign of an inevitable downward spiral. Doing badly on an exam was not just one test grade but evidence of a slippery slope down to where he and my mother felt they resided. The consequences of my not succeeding were ripe to him in a way that I could not understand.

So when I nearly failed an economics class my junior year of high school, he started screaming soon after he saw the report card. He brought me out to our backyard and pointed to a large, empty black pot that had once held a small tree inside of our house.

He told me to pick it up and when I said it was too heavy he got close to my face and screamed that if I did not pick up this plant pot, if I did not hold it in my arms, he would beat the shit out of me. And so I picked it up.

Don't you dare fucking drop it, he said. And so I didn't.

I stood there, shifting the weight of the pot from one arm and a lifted knee to the other, sweating and crying.

Our yard—two hundred fifty square feet of uneven concrete—doubled as a parking space after my parents poured cement on the curb to make a ramp and built swinging gates that opened up to the street. It was a not-so-legal last resort to stop our car tires from being stolen and the windows smashed. For a while before that we had a car that my parents bought for $110 because they figured if it got stolen it was no big deal. It got stolen.

A cherry tree grew out of the lone space of dirt at the cracked intersections of concrete. My parents had planted it when I was a toddler, not expecting much, but it just kept growing—its branches reached over the gate so fully that people walking by could pluck off cherries without breaking their stride. Every year my sister and I watched for the cherries—the greening of the branches, then the white flowers, then the fruit—and fought over who would climb highest on the ladder to pick the "best" ones without any bruises.

The tree started producing more cherries than my parents knew what to do with—one or two hundred pounds a year—so my father filled brown paper lunch bags up with them and gave cherries out to neighbors, shop owners, or anyone who stopped to look at the tree. *You like the cherries? Take a bag!*

My father joked that the shade from the tree, which reached over onto the sidewalk, made it "romantic" for the men who parked there with prostitutes. Once, though, when a cabdriver was getting a blow job as we were walking outside one Sunday afternoon, my dad started beating on his car hood. *Get the fuck out of here! There are kids here, get the fuck out!*

I had been holding the plant pot for a little over an hour, I think, when my father walked out of the sliding glass doors and yelled for me to put the plant pot down and get into our car. He drove for a short bit and parked in front of a large factory building that took up almost the whole block. It looked closed down, but the windows were propped open with phone books and sticks. He told me that it only took a few mistakes to end up working in a place like this. That if I didn't take advantage of all that he and my mother had built for us, I could slip, easily, into something else.

And so I did my best not to fail at things, but when I inevitably did I worked even harder to cover those failures up. I knew my dad loved me but I also knew he loved my successes just as much. That they filled something up for him that I could not on my own.

It was for the same reason, I imagine, that my father talked me out of every waitressing and bartending job I thought about getting throughout college and in my early twenties. He told me that it was easy, when you had real money in your pocket, to just quit school because the alternative was so seductive. The part-time jobs I had in the mall or at his store selling older women clothing and lingerie, I suppose, seemed less dangerous to him.

And though I couldn't imagine a future in which I would quit school to wait tables—it was so far from the reality my parents had carefully cultivated for me—for them, for him, it was just one bad choice around the corner. But my family and aunts and uncles and cousins were made up of waitresses and butchers and a few people who worked in offices because my uncle—the only person in my family to have gone to college, night school in Queens for years—got them the job. I didn't see anything wrong with that, with being like my family, but I knew to my parents there could be nothing worse. That these were not considered acceptable choices. I knew that what I did, what I accomplished, was not just about me. Maybe not at all about me.

And so I did what I was supposed to do—embody the things my parents had wished for themselves, sometimes even against my better judgment.

DURING A SUMMER TRIP AS A CHILD TO VISIT MY GRANDFATHER and step-grandmother in Florida, my father made a mistake. We were going to the beach every day, and on one of the mornings the sand was littered with the blue and white puffed-up corpses of jellyfish of varying sizes.

I was a good swimmer but the sheer number of the dead bodies on the beach scared me, and I didn't want to go in the water. My father tells me that he took me on a long walk that day along the beach, telling me about how important it was to go ahead and do things even when you're afraid. That I didn't need to worry so much, that I should go in. That there were no jellyfish in the water. And so I swam.

I was only in the water a few minutes, of course, before I felt a stinging on my leg moving up my thigh. When I came out on the beach my leg was bright red and swelling and I yelled at my father that he promised I wouldn't get stung.

It made for a good story for my classmates when I got home though, and the jellyfish—which I had never really seen, just felt—got bigger every time I repeated the story to a new friend.

THERE SIMPLY CAME A POINT WHERE THE KNOWLEDGE MY father had wasn't enough to help me anymore. It happened around high school, I think, when my parents couldn't talk to me about my homework. Later, when it came time to research schools and apply to colleges, in a way I was worse off with them than I would have been on my own.

Their advice was based entirely on what they wanted so badly for me rather than what was possible. And because I wanted to please them so much, I didn't fight hard enough to tell them anything other than what they wanted to hear.

That's how I found myself taking tours of colleges completely out of my reach—schools like Wesleyan, where my father wanted me to go so badly that he had me visit twice, the second time to have an informal interview with a student leader who might recommend me. I mumbled and blushed my way through our conversation—I had never met a person close to my age who spoke so much like an adult.

In the end, they were satisfied when I decided on Tulane over a handful of other decent colleges that had accepted me. Despite its distance, when my parents saw the campus buildings and ivy and grass, it looked to them the way they imagined colleges were supposed to look, and so they were happy and proud.

When my father had a heart attack during my winter break a few months later, he made me promise as the doctors worked on him that I would stay in college. I went out to the parking lot and smoked a cigarette. I was already on academic probation, hardly going to class, and knew that I could not tell him.

All of my successes were his successes, but all of my failures were mine alone and I didn't want to sit with that thing by myself. And so I said nothing. I went back to school, but not to classes, and told my parents I would not be going back my sophomore year. They convinced me to drive to Albany, New York, where I enrolled as a nonmatriculated student at the SUNY there and moved into the dorms for transfer students, small rooms with metal-frame twin beds and a tiny square refrigerator under the window. Even there, I couldn't quite get it together.

I met boys and drank often, skipped class and lied to my parents. It took me two years to find my footing but I managed, just barely, to graduate. I couldn't bring myself to go to the graduation ceremony so I went to the smaller informal reception for English majors, wearing a spaghetti-strap dress rather than a graduation gown. We drove to Woodstock later that afternoon with my then-boyfriend to celebrate with a dinner.

A few years ago, my parents realized they couldn't afford to stay in our house in Queens but that young hip families would pay a lot of rent to live there. And so they moved into a small apartment in Astoria that used to be mine, their furniture cramped into the tiny rooms pushed up against the walls. Around the same time, the cherry tree in our yard started to die, disease crawling up the trunk, resulting in fewer and fewer cherries. They didn't tell me when they chopped it down—I saw the hacked stump when I dropped by one day to peek over the fence to see what the house looked like without us in it.

It looked smaller than I remembered.

BOYS

THE COUCH DOWNSTAIRS WAS THE BEST PLACE TO HOOK UP. THE open, no-walls setup of our house may have given my parents the feeling that nothing *that* bad could have gone on under their noses after they went upstairs to sleep, their bedroom right above us. But the benefit of living in a loftlike space with your parents is that you can always see them coming.

And so the couch in the living room became the place that I would "watch movies" with boys late into the night, my head on the side of the couch that could look up the open staircase to watch for any movement above.

The first time I had sex, though, it was in a small room in a walk-up apartment in a three-family building in Park Slope, Brooklyn. My boyfriend Jay's parents worked until early evening so we always had the place to ourselves after school. After it was done—fish-printed boxers put back on, a Gap red hoodie slipped back over my head—Jay wrote our initials in a heart and the date on the underside of a shelf that hung over his bed so that only the person who was lying on it could see.

We went to his house most days because Brooklyn was closer to our school, which was in Tribeca, than my house in Queens was. We took the F train to 7th Avenue and 9th Street and walked a few blocks out of the way when going to Jay's house because there was a group of boys from the neighborhood that kept robbing and hassling him on the way home.

His best friend and my best friend introduced us; their families spent summers together at the same colony in upstate New York. I was thirteen years old and a freshman and I didn't understand what a summer colony was but thought it sounded rich. He was a junior and fine looking but awkward in the way that all sixteen-year-old boys are—he had braces and hair parted down the middle that was a bit floppy but the supreme confidence of someone much cooler. He tagged mailboxes and subway walls with graffiti, or a sticker with his tag already scrawled across it in black marker if he needed to be fast.

I BECOME A MASTER IN THE ART OF UNDER-THE-PANTS HAND jobs. I think of them as a distraction from the months-long campaign from Jay on why we should have sex (mostly because he doesn't want to be a virgin when he turns seventeen years old). Besides, seeing so many penises on the subways, limp and ridiculous looking, does not make me keen on looking at his up close. The idea that someone I love actually has one seems kind of appalling. So I do all I can to hook up and be a good girlfriend without facing it.

I expect to feel different after sex but don't. Even the act itself is somewhat underwhelming. Just painful, mostly. Jay's friend calls in the middle of it and laughs when he realizes what is happening on the other end of the line. I ask Jay to hurry up, over and over, because I want it to stop. It gets better, eventually. A few times later.

Beforehand, as it becomes clearer that I am finally going to just get it over with already, I go with Jay to a clinic that I found out about through a friend—a place where I can go and have my first gyno appointment and get birth control pills without its showing up on my parents' insurance. The exam itself isn't as unpleasant as I thought it would be—I am mostly just glad that it is a woman doctor—and they give me six months' worth of birth control pills for free. All I have to do, she says, is come back again and she would give me more for a few dollars a pack. I feel adult, but shamed a few months later when my then-twelve-year-old sister tells me that my mother had found the pills and started weeping immediately. She had always told me to go to her if I wanted birth control, that I could talk to her about it, and I am thankful that I had realized it had always been a well-meaning lie.

Jay always seems concerned about where I was and whether I was lying about where I was. Once, when we are supposed to meet somewhere downtown but the trains were delayed and I couldn't find a working pay phone to beep him, he accuses me of making up the train delay to cover for the fact that I was late. And probably somewhere else, he thought. His cousin tells me that Jay had planned to tell me that he called the MTA and that they told him there was not a train delay to see how I reacted. To catch me in a lie. I don't know why he decides not to.

For Valentine's Day, he gets me a beeper. The translucent blue pager comes in a tie box wrapped in tissue paper and filled with candy hearts with cute phrases on them. This way, he says, he could always be in touch with me.

We fought a lot, and so when I go out to a club with my friends in midtown in my sophomore year, I make out with a boy on the dance floor who goes to Bronx Science. He is just an okay kisser but a lot nicer than Jay. Taller, too. We talk on the phone for a few weeks while he tries to convince me to break up with my boyfriend. We do break up, a few weeks later, and I try to lead Jay to believe that this is his idea.

I continue to go out with my Science friends on the weekends, smoking pot behind their buildings before we take a cab to the "club"—a Chippendales during the week that switches over to a teenage party on the weekends. My parents allow me to go if a friend or a friend of a friend is "promoting"—a fancy way of saying you get people to show up and your name goes on a flyer. I can stay until midnight or one a.m., when my parents drive over to pick me up a block away so no one sees me get in their car.

Jay calls me to tell me about sleeping with another girl and that all he could think about the whole time was how he had to pee. I tell my Science boy that I can't be his girlfriend, that we are just "seeing" each other, but I still meet his mother over dinner one night on the Upper West Side.

Once Jay found out about the relationship, whatever it was, things changed quickly. He wants to get back together desperately. First he broke into my locker and left an envelope with "Lies . . ." scrawled across it—in it was every note or letter I'd ever written him. When that didn't work he'd break in and leave flowers or—one time—a blown-up picture of himself with his arms outstretched. When I finally agreed to take him back he made me bring in the mix tape that the boy from Bronx Science had made me. He stomped on it with his foot until it cracked, then pulled out the tape from the cassette.

I met Jack two and a half years later, after Jay left for college and started dating a girl with a lip ring who recorded a message for his answering machine that sounded like she was having an orgasm: *Jay . . . isn't, oh my god, here right now, yes yes . . .*

Jack was the most beautiful guy I had seen up close. We meet in Saugerties, New York, at a barbecue where he is grilling in a tank top and jeans, all muscles and smiles, with a shamrock tattoo on his shoulder. It is his twentieth birthday and at sixteen I am the youngest person there, but I am also from New York, which seems to even the disparity out. I cannot stop staring at him.

We don't speak at all, but the following day he calls me to ask me to the movies—the first time I've been asked on a proper date—and I am thrilled. I don't remember what we see but after the show he drives me home and we sit on my parents' couch in their house in Woodstock and we talk until two a.m., until finally he kisses me. I only have a month left upstate before my senior year starts, and so we spend every day together and within a week Jack tells me he's in love with me. I tell my parents he is eighteen.

My father is horrified by Jack, who does not go to college but instead works the desk at a gym near his house, taking on occasional clients as a personal trainer. He asks me what I see in him and I respond, giddy, *Have you seen him?!*

Jack is six foot three and chiseled—like in a movie star or stripper way. He let me take shirtless pictures of him in the shower, hand up against the wall, posing. A few months before we met he got head shots so he can try to model or act. He works out for hours every day. Because we are in love he decides to move in with his father, who lives in Queens, to pursue whatever career these photos might bring.

Before we leave Woodstock that summer to go back to New York, though, my mother—after going through my backpack—finds a small pipe for smoking pot and a few condoms. She says she wants to take me for a walk to talk about sex but I refuse. She screams that no one will ever want to marry me if I keep having sex with boys. When she grounds me, I realize it is for the condoms and not the marijuana. She denies it. She says we'll keep the grounding a secret from my father, and I'm not sure if it's because he'll be seriously mad and she's protecting me or because he'll find my offenses mundane and she's protecting herself and her authority over me.

Back in New York, I bring Jack to every school dance I can, every house party. My guy friends, scrawny in comparison, are impressed but a little afraid of him when he gets drunk and belligerent. One night when I have a party at my house he punches a screen out of an upstairs window. On another night he fills the tub up and holds his head under the water until I agree to stop fighting with him.

To an outsider, a sixteen-year-old girl dating a twenty-year-old man seems like a bad idea. It mostly is. But Jack was naïve, and I was more in control than he was. And though he gave me my first taste of hard liquor (Goldschläger) and towered above everyone I knew, I was thrilled by him. I remember noticing the outline of his body the first time he got on top of me—huge and muscular—and thinking that this is what fucking a man is like. There were no scrawny arms or adolescent halfhearted facial hair, just girth.

One time in his room, though—an enclosed patio that his mother turned into a bedroom for him—the sex feels different. When I go to the bathroom afterward, the top half of a condom falls out from inside of me. My dancer girlfriend takes control and tells me she will call around to doctors about a pill she heard you can take after sex to make sure you don't get pregnant. She calls it *postcoitus medication* so when I go to the doctor that my friend found for me, I write the same thing in the space where it says *Reason for visit*. It is the first time I have had a male gynecologist and I start to panic until I realize that he is going to have the nurse stay in the room the entire time.

The medication makes me throw up a bit, but I am otherwise fine, and Jack cannot believe that I pulled this off by myself.

After about seven months of dating, though, he stops calling. He doesn't show up at my house when he says he's going to. Despite my bluster to friends about having a trophy boyfriend I am devastated when, finally, he tells me over the phone that he wants to break up. That the attraction was just physical and there is nothing really beyond that.

My friends, being kind, help me to make a list of the reasons it's actually excellent news that he doesn't want us to be together, including that he shaves his legs and testicles, uses women's deodorant, and won't give head. We spend the day—senior cut day—on the Columbia University campus uptown, pretending to be students and smoking pot. After we're as high as we want to be we go to Tom's diner on the corner of 112th Street and Broadway and order fries and mozzarella sticks.

I spend the rest of the school year, my last in high school, smoking pot and hooking up with friends of mine—though no one seems quite as adult or good-looking as Jack. On the day that our yearbooks come out I notice that my girlfriends have taken out an ad together, congratulating each other and posing with each other in a box that takes up a quarter of the page. Soon after a male friend tells me that they've planned a trip to Europe together for the summer before college and asked people not to tell me about it because they thought it was better that way.

So I work at my parents' store in Queens and pack up my bedroom that used to be a closet.

COLLEGE

BEFORE PAUL AND I BREAK UP, I HAVE A DREAM THAT I'M FLOAT-
ing slowly upward into the sky, able to do so because of a small
green olive in my hand. Paul is on the ground, beneath me, and
I keep handing him pieces of the olive, bit after bit, so he can
float with me. Soon, though, all I have left is the pit—Paul has
all of the small green pieces crumbling in his hand. But still, he
stays grounded.

I met Paul nearly four years earlier through my drug dealer,
a tall rich kid who lived in my dorm in Albany—my second-try
college—and sold ecstasy and weed. I was with a friend, danc-
ing in the basement of a bar that had been turned into a "club"
with thrown-up dance-floor lights and some palm leaves to
cover the walls as you walked down the stairs. My friend wore a
light blue velour shirt because we thought it would feel good to
the touch once we started rolling, and it did, and soon after we
ran into Lou to ask him for more pills.

He introduced me to Paul, who was almost exactly my

height at five foot five, and had reddish hair. I joked that I had never met a redheaded Italian before and he showed me how if he held a lighter under a Vicks inhaler and then blew the smoke in my face, I would bliss out for a few seconds as the menthol hit my throat and eyes.

We slept together that night, talking until four a.m. and eating Oreo cookies in the dorm room he shared one floor below my own. Later he would move into a room on my floor, taking the place of a guy I let go down on me once to prove he was as good as he said he was. (He was fine.) Paul came to see me the next day at my job at the dorm building administrative office, bringing Gatorade and more Oreos. We became a couple immediately.

Paul is from the Bronx but his parents moved him to Westchester when they thought he was getting into too much trouble in New York City. We connect over transferring to a new college, our Italian borough backgrounds, and being smart but not knowing quite what to do with ourselves.

We drive constantly and spend more time in Paul's car than anywhere else: from Albany to New York, New York to Westchester, Westchester to Woodstock, Woodstock to Albany. One night the engine of his car seizes and we have to stay in a motel off the throughway that takes Paul's mom's credit card number written on a napkin as payment. We have no cash on us and the only thing we have to eat is the candy necklace I bought at a rest stop, so we take the pieces off the elastic string and make a tent in between the two beds in the room because sleeping on the floor seems more fun, and clean, than sleeping on the sheets in this motel.

On another ride we are on the Taconic and I'm giving Paul head as he drives and we get pulled over by a cop because he's swerving, but we don't get a ticket, we never get tickets, because Paul keeps his dad's business card—he's an NYPD carpenter—on the dash. He also managed to pull up his pants, but not button them, before the cop came to the window. We laugh about it for the rest of the trip.

His mom collects ducks and apples and one night while we are high on either weed or E we decide to count the number of apples—on the wallpaper, as salt and pepper shakers, as magnets, and as fake fruit in a bowl. We get to one hundred before we give up.

By senior year we move in together, into a five-hundred-dollar-a-month one-bedroom apartment on Albany's Madison Avenue, in between a run-down bar and the state museum. Paul gets me a kitten that we name Neidra after mishearing our yoga teacher talk about yoga nidra. In the summers he works at a grocery store and I stay in New York as a teacher's assistant for preschoolers in summer camp. During the school year, we work at the Albany mall in adjoining stores to help pay the bills: me at the Body Shop, selling lotions and perfumes to older women and nervous boyfriends, him at Lids, selling baseball hats to other college students.

We inadvertently buy the same pair of New Balance sneakers and even though his are "men's" and mine are "women's" our shoes sizes are similar enough that we sometimes mistake one pair for the other and wear each other's shoes. When I start taking women's studies classes, and loving them, he is happy. We take Shakespeare classes together and he tells me he would like to be a teacher though his family wants him to get a business degree. He spills his coffee on himself every morning. We do coke with one of my women's studies professors in her house when we cannot get ecstasy.

I am in a rhythm where I feel I have found my place, finally.

I ONLY WENT TO CLASSES EVERY ONCE IN A WHILE AT MY FIRST college, Tulane University in New Orleans. I was seventeen years old, away from home for the first time, and not quite sure what I was supposed to be doing. I followed the girls on my hall to parties and the classes we shared, wondering why they wore pajama pants outside and wishing I was home.

My only experience with what college was supposed to be like came from movies, so I was shocked when the new friends I made on my dorm room floor started to rush sororities. I thought this was only something that super-wealthy snobby girls did. They came home from rush activities complaining that their faces hurt from smiling so much and that they were behind on studying. But still, they hoped that they would all get into the same sorority. Paying for friends, I said, seems pathetic. Besides, it was more money than I could afford. Still, even though my parents had helped me to set up a job for a few hours a week on campus to help pay for books—working at a day-care center—I gave up when I couldn't find the building that first week. I was too embarrassed to ask anyone for help.

I wrote a letter to my mother and father on my roommate's computer, printing it out and mailing it, telling them that this place didn't feel like the real world. That when you walked into the cafeteria, it was racially segregated by table and that some of the girls in my dorm didn't even live there—that their parents were renting apartments for them close by. I wrote to them that most everyone drank every night and that the classes were harder than I expected. I told them it was clear to me that I didn't belong there. That maybe I should come home. Years later, I found this letter tucked away in a box of my father's along with birthday cards I'd given him and drawings from when I was a child. *We thought all kids at college were homesick*, he said.

Kyle wouldn't have been my first choice for a boyfriend. His smile was more like a sideways smirk, his thick Boston accent was grating, and—as if he'd walked off the set for a nineties frat movie—he was always wearing the same dirty white hat. But he also had big arms and a great sense of humor, so when he asked me to see a football game I said yes. I was happy to be included in something that seemed so college-y.

Just as friends, he said. *You're not my type.*

Getting an official date for the party before Tulane's game was part of his fraternity's rush activities. Each pledge needed to show up with someone and since we joked around with each other in Latin class, both sarcastic East Coasters in a private Southern university, he thought it seemed like a good match.

I borrowed a brown spaghetti-strap dress from a girl down the hall, pinned my hair back with a pink rhinestone bobby pin, and teetered over in terrible black pumps to the ATM near the center of campus where we planned to meet, even though we lived in the same dorm. I could tell, when he looked at me, that he was pleased.

I don't recall much about the date other than he got wasted and spilled nacho cheese all over the borrowed brown dress as we sat in the bleachers. I rode back to campus on a bus with some other girls whose dates had gotten similarly obliterated. It occurs to me now that the bus must have been there for just that reason.

Kyle taught me how to throw up when I got too drunk early in the evening so I could continue to drink more, and brought me to the fifty-cent drink nights (Tuesdays) and "penny pitcher" nights (Wednesdays), so we were out nearly every night drinking and, soon, fucking.

I had never met anyone who wanted to have sex so often, a few times a day at least—most of the time in his dorm room, just a floor down from my own, and sometimes in the boys' shower, where he had to go in first to check to see if anyone was there or if someone had, as they had more than once, taken a shit on the shower floor. I also had never met anyone whose penis was so large that when he got an erection it didn't stand straight up, but instead stood out perpendicular to his body, too heavy to make it all the way up.

I knew that he kept porn in several shoe boxes under his bed—magazines and tapes, most of which had to do with asses and anal sex—but he assured me that all men had this amount of pornography and it was all for fun anyway, even though I did not like the pained look on some of the women's faces.

His roommate, a boy from Pennsylvania who went to boarding school with Kyle, drank the most out of any of us. He also smoked pot quite a bit in the room, rolling up towels to line the crack at the bottom of the door so the RA wouldn't catch on and sometimes blowing the smoke through a toilet paper tube with a dryer sheet rubber-banded to the end. One night Kyle and I woke up to his peeing on us, sleepwalking. I could not stop laughing but Kyle was furious, and wet—the urine soaked through the egg-crate mattress topper and so he needed to sleep in my room. He hated coming to my room.

Kyle had a hard time rushing his fraternity. He wasn't really keeping his grades up enough and though he wanted to be part of the frat that was known on campus as the heaviest drinking, the hardest partying, he was more aggressive than most of the men there. He got in fights more often. The other guys on his floor were afraid of him; they avoided him when he got drunk. One asked why I would want to date him.

My friends were skeptical of Kyle; at one point a girl on my floor sat me down with her roommate to tell me that a few nights previous, while drunk, he had tried to kiss her. When confronted, Kyle simply said she was a lying slut. Another friend made a similar claim but I insisted he was too drunk to understand what he was doing. Soon he started to pick at me. I cursed too much; girls shouldn't curse that much. Why did I expect to have an orgasm every time we had sex? That seemed greedy.

One night, when his roommate had some friends over, I was joking around with them—being sarcastic, silly. Kyle was furious and accused me of humiliating him by not showing him the proper respect a girlfriend should. When I asked if he was actually saying I shouldn't talk to other men, even as friends, he answered quickly: *yes*. He got drunk most nights, tried to start fights with other men often. Still, when he crawled into bed with me, he wept about missing home and his family, and told me about being adopted—something, he said, he had never told anyone. He told me he felt weak.

But when we went home for Christmas break, he didn't call. Even after my father had a heart attack and I called him at home, crying, he only stayed on the phone for a few minutes before telling me he needed to do something for his mom. We broke up the first day back from break, and I found out he had invited another girl—a girl in a sorority—to his first official fraternity trip to Florida. He wanted to have sex once more before we made our breakup official, which I was fine with, and when he was done I asked him if I was ever really his girlfriend.

One of his friends who lived on our floor told me that he broke up with me because I got too fat over the course of the first semester, and because I was too "mouthy." *He said you had anal sex too*, this friend said, smiling. I insisted that was a lie, which it was, but his friend replied that it was okay if I didn't want to admit it—*it was a pretty nasty thing to do.*

Despite my best efforts I had not been able to get drunk the first two nights of Mardi Gras week—just barely buzzed despite drinking as much as Kyle taught me to. So my friends and I bought Boone's Strawberry Hill and each drank a bottle and then funneled Jack Daniel's until we were spitting it up onto the gray dorm room floors.

We went to a bar called the Boot that was so close to campus it might as well have been on it, beads on our necks, carrying whatever was left of the Jack Daniel's. I don't remember much. I know the crowd was huge and that I saw Kyle's roommate there. As a song was ending he kissed me, and I let him. I know we had sex, that I asked him to please not tell Kyle, and that he answered by laughing.

I made it back to my room somehow and woke up a few hours later when I heard Kyle screaming outside of my door for me to come out. I didn't want him to wake up my roommate and so I went into the hallway in my pajamas and sat with my back against the door to my room. He stood over me, telling me I was the dirtiest piece of trash he could imagine.

You're a piece-of-shit garbage whore, do you understand that? I didn't answer, but I didn't think he was really looking for me to. *I can't even stand to look at you because of how filthy you are. You're a garbage person, you smell, do you know that? You're fucking trash*

*and I don't want to ever fucking see you again because I don't fuck-
ing associate with whores.* He went on like this for a while, maybe
five or ten minutes, before leaving. I didn't say anything, I just
sat. I remember being surprised that no one came out of their
room, if not to help, then because of the noise.

In the middle of the night I heard multiple men outside of my
door. *Open up, whore!* one said. I recognized one of the voices
as a friend of mine who also knew Kyle. I put my pillow over
my head. In the morning I found a condom taped to the front of
my door with what looked like semen inside of it. WHORE was
written across the door's dry-erase board in marker. It may have
been SLUT. I don't remember the word, just the definition. As if
the condom wasn't clear enough.

A few days later when I was walking across campus one of
Kyle's fraternity brothers, someone I had never met but knew
by his reputation for hooking up with freshmen, stopped me as
I was crossing a piece of grassy field in front of one of the ivy-
covered buildings. *I hear you like it in the ass*, he said. I stayed
silent and tried to move around him, but he shifted his weight to
one side so I couldn't. *Maybe you'd like it from me.* As I walked
away he spat on the piece of grass I had just been standing on.

I called my father, and while I didn't tell him the whole story
I did tell him about the condom taped to my door and about
hooking up with Kyle's roommate. He told me it would be fine.
It could have been a lot worse, he said. *When boys get to that place
they can do really bad things.* I was lucky.

I stopped leaving my room during the day. I didn't go to

class and ignored the mailed warnings that arrived in my campus box. I knew I did not want to be there next year.

Spring was rainy but beautiful in New Orleans. I spent more time walking around the neighborhood that surrounded the campus than going to class, dodging the buck moth caterpillars that fell from the trees. They were plump and cute but their stings hurt like hell.

I heard a rumor that Kyle's parents had shown up at the dorm. They found out that he was failing classes and so they pulled him out, putting all of his things in the back of their car and not even giving him a chance to say good-bye to anyone. When I expressed my relief to one of my girlfriends on the floor, she scowled at me. *It's shitty*, she says, *to take pleasure in someone else's pain.*

Before I left at the end of the semester I got a letter saying that if I wanted to stay enrolled I would need to take summer classes to make up for all the ones that I skipped in the spring. I threw it away and told my parents that I wanted to transfer— leaving out that I didn't have much of a choice.

FRIENDS MAKE FUN OF PAUL AND ME FOR BEING *BASICALLY married* while in college but we are far from perfect. I am far from perfect. One day while we are at Paul's house in Westchester, he plays video games with his youngest brother, sitting on the floor in front of the bed that belongs to his middle brother. His middle brother and I are lying on our stomachs, heads propped up by our hands, also watching. At some point, this brother slides his hand over and puts it on my ass. I don't move my eyes from the screen; I don't say anything. I'm not sure what to do so I do nothing and let him leave it there, though I think I remember his rubbing me at one point. He is seventeen years old. I am flattered but also frozen.

We catch up over a dinner years later, and Paul tells me that despite his support of my bourgeoning feminism I got drunk one night and yelled at him when he tried to pick me up off the floor, saying something about not needing a man. I'm not sure if this is the memory of a person who has caricaturized what a feminist might do or the actions of a drunken idiot newly finding her politics, but either case does not seem very flattering to me. I am either an asshole or someone that a person remembers as an asshole.

I WOULD LIKE TO SAY THAT BEING WITH SOMEONE WHO LEGITImately loved and respected me brought out the best in me but the truth is that anything good that Paul gave to me I rejected. I know that I loved him—he's probably the only person other than my husband for whom I really think that's true—but I treated him poorly, still. I'm sure I was a good girlfriend in many ways (see: road head, above) but although I was drawn to someone who treated me as his equal, I did not know what to do with that gift.

That I thought it was a gift rather than a given was probably the problem.

Being treated nicely felt wrong somehow, as if we were acting out what a relationship should be rather than being in it. For men who hate women, an admission like this one is proof that *see, women want a guy who treats them like shit* but that's not true either. What is closer to the truth is that when confronted with the love you deserve, it is easier to mock it than accept it. Especially when everything else you have experienced of love and connection is based on something more like control or disdain. That is part of the reason I ended up with my husband. I loved him, yes—passionately and fully. But I also recognized at some point that loving him was a good choice. It took me a while to get there.

Before we moved out of our apartment in Albany—heading back to New York so Paul could move back in with his parents and look for jobs and I could move in with a friend and apply to graduate school—our cat, scared by the noise and disappearing furniture, snuck behind the stove and into a hole in the wall. Neidra ran far in and couldn't figure out how to get back out. As friends helped us move, she stayed in the wall—for hours, I think. Paul sat by the wall, calling to her, reaching in occasionally, trying to lure her with treats and then, finally, tuna fish.

We decided that I would keep her, but one night when my roommate got drunk she slammed the door on Neidra's tail— amputating most of it and skinning the rest. My roommate didn't realize the harm she'd caused, she said, but when I got home there was blood all over the apartment and I had to rush the cat in to get surgery to remove the rest of her tail. She stayed with Paul for a while after that.

We had talked about getting married but he wanted to live near his parents; he wanted a housewife, I thought, and wasn't interested enough to ask which graduate programs I was applying to. He wanted a calm sort of life. And so we broke up, not long after the dream about olives; I told him that we wanted different things.

Later we would sleep together when he was seeing other women, when I was seeing other men. It was easy to have a drink or go to dinner and by the end we would be holding hands again, looking at each other as if we were still in college. In a way I think I wished we were.

So when I told him, years later, that I thought we should give it another try it did not surprise me that he responded by saying that his mother never thought I would be good with kids. That I would work too much and not be willing to be a stay-at-home mom. It felt as if he had been waiting to hurt me with something for a while, maybe deservedly.

He married someone—smart, blond, pretty—who wanted the same things that he did. They bought a house in the same town as his parents and had two kids. He seems happy.

GRILLED CHEESE

THE DAY AFTER HE FUCKED ME WHILE I WAS UNCONSCIOUS, I HAD Carl buy me a grilled cheese sandwich and french fries.

I had gone to his apartment the night before with my sister because he was having a few friends over and she had nothing else going on. She left early in the evening and I got drunker than usual faster than usual. The next morning, I woke up confused and with ten missed calls from my parents. I was naked.

When I joked to him about date-raping me, he shot back: *Don't worry, I went down on you first.*

I DON'T REMEMBER HOW OR WHERE I MET CARL, BUT I IMAGINE IT must have been at a bar, and it must have been in midtown because he worked in finance and there were none of those types in Williamsburg yet. I also don't remember liking him much, which doesn't say a lot for my taste or mind-set at the time.

Carl wasn't great-looking or particularly charming, but he had a decent sense of humor and I was bored and dating a lot.

So even though he had visible blackheads in his ear and I found him somewhat disgusting in bed—all sweat and freckles—I kept seeing him.

Whenever I spent the night at his place—a high-rise in Manhattan overlooking the river—he would give me money for cab fare home. It was often more than I needed and I could never figure out if I thought this was gentlemanly or if it made me feel like a prostitute.

He came to visit me in Brooklyn once, to look at the loft I had just rented with a girl I used to intern with and her boyfriend. It was huge and illegal, like any decent apartment in Williamsburg in 2002. I had to bring one month's rent in cash for the building manager as a "down payment" that I would never see again before we could move in. Then I had to pay the building super extra to build walls for bedrooms.

I took Carl to my favorite bar in the neighborhood, a place on Bedford Avenue, but he wanted to leave quickly. *That was weird*, he said. When I asked what he meant he said he felt like a "cracker" because we were the only white people at the bar—which I'm pretty sure wasn't true and I thought was such a strange thing to notice in any case. I had never heard anyone use the term "cracker" before in a way that suggested anything but irony.

After that we stopped talking. For months, I think. I don't know how long it had been. I do know I hadn't seen Carl in a while when he invited me to come over to his apartment for a small party.

That night at his place, where the only other partygoers were a small group of his male friends, I found out that he'd told them that I was bisexual, which I was not. My sister, confused, had heard them talking about it and came up to ask me if I was and for whatever reason had decided not to tell her. I wonder if it just made what he thought was a good story for his friends. Finance bro dates Williamsburg feminist. "Possible bisexual" could have added to the allure, I guess.

Normally I could handle my booze, and I don't remember drinking much, but I know my sister left, I said I was staying, and then I woke up to Carl taking off my clothes. Briefly, I thought it was sweet—he was undressing me for bed because I was too drunk to do it myself.

I don't know much about what happened next. I know I remember asking what he was doing when I realized he was on top of me. Then nothing. I don't know if I said *Don't do this*, or if I said *That's nice*, or if I said nothing, which seems the most likely possibility given my state.

I do know I was upset. I know when I woke up the next afternoon—I had slept until two p.m.—I said you're not supposed to have sex with someone who is passed out. I know I was still drunk when I said this. I joked. I made a joke about *uh isn't that date rape?*, saying it in a way that seemed ribbing or sarcastic; I'm not sure why. That's when he smiled and promised me that he ate me out first.

Then I told him if he was going to fuck me while I was unconscious the least he could do was order a grilled cheese and french fries from the delivery place so I could soak up some of the previous night's alcohol. I know I waited for the food to come and ate it before I left. I know I called my parents to apologize for worrying them. I know I cried when I got home.

I have never called this assault. I'm not really sure why. As a feminist writer I've encouraged others to name the thing that happened to them so our stories can be laid bare in a way that is inescapable and impossible to argue with. And I realize, and I realized then, that by definition penetrating someone while they are unconscious—even if you've had sex before with this person—is rape. I just have never wanted to call it that.

The truth is that this thing that happened, no matter what you want to call it, did not have a lasting impact on me, and for that I feel . . . strange.

It did not destroy me or change who I am in the way I thought something like that is supposed to. I don't still think about Carl or that night. I don't carry scars from it. On the scale of things that have happened to me, things that have hurt me and damaged me, this registered lower than finding a stranger had ejaculated on the back of my jeans on the subway. I don't know why.

I know that my shameful uncertainty likely has to do with the fact that I did not feel like a person who was capable of being violated because at the time I barely considered myself a person. I was wandering in and out of relationships as frequently as I was walking in and out of bars and jobs and friendships. I remember taking the subway listening to music a lot and narrating to myself as if I was watching a movie about a girl with headphones in her ears walking through subway tunnels.

I want to be unequivocal because my politics call for it and because I know that by not doing so I am opening myself up to criticism on all sides. I know that if any young woman told me this same story I would not hesitate to call it what it is. I don't know why I don't allow myself the same courtesy. Maybe I'm just exhausted of feeling like an arbiter of sexual violence, even for myself.

I have had men accused of rape come up to me at colleges after I've spoken there, looking for some sort of absolution and for me to tell them that this thing they did was not rape even though I was not there and I have no idea.

One young man followed me around a reception after a speech I gave at a Midwestern college insisting that I give him an answer as to whether lying to someone about something important—he would not say what—and having sex with them under these false pretenses was rape. For a friend, he said.

He would not take my *I can't answer that* as an answer and even when I told him I didn't want to talk with him anymore, he kept following me around the room, which told me a lot more about the possible answer to his question than the actual circumstances he described.

Another told me he had been kicked out of his previous school after being found guilty of rape but he did not do it. I don't know what to say to these men, these possible rapists, who want something from me, because I have nothing to give.

I never saw Carl again. We never spoke after I left his apartment after eating my grilled cheese and french fries. He did give me cab money, though. And I know that I took it.

WILLIAMSBURG

I KNEW IT WAS OVER WHEN INSTEAD OF GETTING ME A RING FOR
Christmas, Ron got me the outline of one. He had been asking
about my ring size all week, which I thought strange because
the idea of this man's proposing—my boyfriend of almost two
years who I thought was cheating on me and I was sure had a
drug problem—seemed impossible. So it's not that I was expecting an engagement ring. I wasn't.

I first met Ron in 2004 in an outdoor bar called the Yabby
that used to be on Bedford Avenue in Brooklyn and is now, I
think, a subpar grocery store. I was drunk when I got there so I
don't remember how we started talking; I might have bummed
a cigarette. I'm almost sure that I did.

My friend Lori and I were there to celebrate the success of a
website we had started together, and we told Ron and his friends
about the party we were having for the site the following night.
We didn't chat for that long, so I was surprised when he showed
up the next night with friends.

Ron was six foot three and broad shouldered, and had blue

eyes. I thought he was fine looking at the time but his somewhat greasy longish hair pulled back in a ponytail gave me pause. He talked to me about feminism and his work as a designer, and flirted mercilessly as we drank more and more. I was wearing a pair of "political" underwear that night that said GIVE BUSH THE FINGER and I surreptitiously lifted my skirt and let him take a few pictures of them as I got drunker. By the time we got back to my apartment it was four a.m. and I could barely walk. So when he pulled out a bag of cocaine, it seemed like a decent idea even though it had been years since I had done any.

Once we were high, we talked about his fucked-up childhood in the South, how as a boy he watched a man hold a knife to his mother's neck, her drug problem, and the fact that he had half brothers and a father he didn't talk to. We didn't have sex until we woke up the following morning. When we did, he didn't even bother taking my underwear off, just pulled them to the side while lying behind me, and when he got on top of me I told him I couldn't take him seriously with all of that hair hanging down into my face.

He called to ask me to dinner a day later, and I repeated my joke again—*I don't know, I really don't like long hair*. Still, I agreed to meet him at a wine bar on the corner of N. 7th and Wythe Avenue. When he showed up, his hair was gone. He had cut it off himself that afternoon and now his reddish-brown hair was close to his head in small waves. The gesture had me so smitten, I didn't mind much when he disappeared for more than a half hour during dinner, *to buy cigarettes*, he said.

We were together immediately, in love within weeks, and the sex was better than any I'd had before. To friends, I likened him to a dirty Ed Burns with a motorcycle. I could not fall fast enough.

His group of friends in the neighborhood were mostly young men whom he knew from design school. They worked at industrial design firms or shoe companies; some were artists on the side, selling their paintings on Bedford Avenue on the weekends. They all were younger than Ron and worshipped him. He was clearly the smartest and most talented of the bunch and had a charisma with people that we discussed often after doing a few lines. We both shared the feeling of not ever being the best-looking person in the room but being the most engaging, the most able to hook up with someone if we wanted to or convince someone of a point over a beer.

Cocaine is not a humble drug.

Soon, every night we went out—two or three evenings a week, at least—involved cocaine. It was as much a part of my evening routine as showering, putting on makeup, or getting a cab. As I got ready for the night out, I had a delivery service bring a bag or two to my apartment. I would do a few bumps off of my house key before meeting Ron at a bar, or if we were going out to dinner, I'd wait until I was done eating to snort some in the bathroom, washing away the drunken feeling that came with the meal's wine. The truth is that I loved coke not so much for the drug itself but because it let me drink as much as I wanted without passing out or embarrassing myself.

It was not a good time, but it was the first time in a long time that I felt something.

When I was high I didn't feel fucked up; I felt present. I could have conversations with people for hours on end without getting distracted and feel like the things I was trying to relay were actually making sense and that I sounded smart. I could finally talk about myself kindly and be proud of the work I was doing—not just thinking it was important but saying so. I didn't take shit from anyone. I was in the moment rather than watching myself from afar. It all felt blustery but true.

Everywhere we went, Ron had friends. He knew every bartender, every drug dealer, every restaurant manager. We never left Williamsburg because we were regulars everywhere. We snorted lines with the bar owners, who loved me for hooking them up with my cute friends, in back rooms and upstairs apartments. The owners and chefs of our favorite restaurants came to the Halloween parties I threw in my loft on N. 3rd Street—an illegal apartment that I now shared with two girls I'd met on Craigslist. Sometimes before the sun rose we would go up to my roof—where we could see Manhattan's full skyline—and just wait for morning, looking at the lights from the city fade.

Work felt like an afterthought. The thing about doing drugs is that if you're privileged enough no one seems to care so long as you can hold yourself together. So long as I showed up to work on time I was a "weekend warrior" even if it was Wednesday and I was still up at seven a.m. considering buying another bag.

One night, a few months in, Ron asked me to marry him while we were having sex. We were high, and it was four or five in the morning, but it didn't feel as unreal as it should have. I told him, *Don't say that*, not to joke about something like that, but he said, with tears in his eyes, that he wasn't joking, that he wanted to be my husband. We never talked about this moment again.

We continued on like this for over a year: having good meals, drinking until four a.m. without getting drunk, and talking until six thirty, doing line after line after line in his friend Ned's basement apartment because it was the darkest even as the sun came up. We had threesomes with his friend's girlfriend, a neighborhood friend, and a Danish woman visiting one of Ron's coworkers. His friends were impressed. We applauded ourselves for our lack of traditional jealousy, scolding others about what true love looked like. It was not possessive; it was not joyless.

Ron took a lot of pride in the fact that I was a feminist and smart. He liked to watch me debate his friends who would insist, noses moist and dripping from too much coke, that rape wasn't that common or that life began at conception. But when it suited him, my feminism became an excuse for him not to do things he didn't feel like doing—if I asked Ron to walk me home at three a.m. he'd say, *But I thought you were a strong feminist*, a common refrain when I needed help to change a tire or, once, asked him to come along to an ultrasound of a lump in my breast.

I started to worry that my nose was going to cave in, that I'd become disfigured and everyone would know what I was doing at night. I favored my right nostril so much that it would always become swollen shut at some point in the night and sometimes stay like that for days.

Sleep became impossible. We covered my bedroom windows—huge factory-style windows that almost reached the ceiling—with dark blankets and sheets, taking Vicodin and drinking beer so that we might finally pass out. I would let the pill dissolve on my tongue for as long as I could take the bitter taste, hoping that somehow this would make it take effect quicker. It never did. When we woke, sometimes not until four or five p.m. the next day, we would order pizza and watch movies as the hangover subsided.

I knew this was all a bad idea, terrible even, in the long run. But in the short term everything seemed to be working out okay. I called in sick a bit too often, that's true, but I had friends, was having fun, was in love, and my website was starting to do really well.

Ron convinced me that I should quit my day job doing communications work at an international women's nonprofit to work on my blog full-time. I loved my job, but it was easy and I was spending work days moderating comments anyway. So I took a consulting job for a DC-based pro-choice organization that would let me work from home, infrequently, for two thousand dollars a month and spent the rest of my time working on the blog and being with Ron.

Excusing his faults became an art. When Ron was late—he was always at least a half hour late to everything, including a birthday dinner that he threw for me—it was only because he needed to feel like he controlled something in his life after having such an uncontrollable experience as a child. The lies he told, about everything from whether he'd taken a taxi or a train to why he'd stood me up yet again, were a product of his trust issues.

I woke up one night with a terrible pain in my abdomen that didn't go away. I asked Ron to take me to the emergency room but he said he was too fucked up—so I called my mother to take me and Ron said he wouldn't be far behind, as soon as he could shower and catch a cab. He didn't answer calls or texts for the rest of the night, and when I finally got home the following morning with a diagnosis of a ruptured ovarian cyst, he was asleep. The reason he didn't come, I told my mother later, was because hospitals terrified him—he saw his own mother taken there often as a child and couldn't bear to be in one himself.

But I remembered how on another night, as I fell asleep on his shoulder in a cab, he took my face into his hands and started kissing my cheeks and forehead softly all over. *I love you,* he said. And when I got into an accident on my scooter—a Vespa-like contraption Ron convinced me I could learn to ride easily—crashing into the street, giving myself road burn all over my arms and legs, and fracturing my hip, he was at my house in under five minutes, saying *baby, poor baby* over and over. He could fix anything from a car to a pair of glasses, he could charm anyone, and when I rode on the back of his motorcycle in the middle of the night looking upward I thought, This is what life is supposed to feel like. *This is what people feel.*

But on Christmas morning, when I opened a ring box in front of my parents that contained *a flat silver ring* with a 2-D silhouette of a diamond on top—as if a real diamond ring had cast a shadow and someone made a ring out of that—I knew it was over. The symbolism was too embarrassing. It was a prop ring, a joke.

Besides, it was becoming clearer that our partying had long turned into something else, something that I could either move away from or linger in with no end date in sight.

That New Year's Eve, Ron had invited our drug dealer to party with us in my apartment along with a small group of friends. We were in my bedroom as the sun was coming up, doing lines off of a hardcover book balancing on my bed, bags strewn about the duvet. I kept putting on more and more blush until my cheeks looked clownish, a fact I didn't notice until after I looked at pictures of that night/morning. It was closing in on six a.m. when, a few feet away from Ron, the dealer told me he would give me coke for free whenever I wanted it if I would just let him eat me out once. Maybe twice.

I told Ron later, horrified, but he shrugged it off as if this was the most expected thing in the world. He thought it was hilarious.

So we stopped seeing each other but kept sleeping together, moving in and out of each other's lives without any sort of official breakup. I stopped doing drugs and asked him to stop as well; he agreed. A few weeks later, when I confronted him with empty baggies found in his jeans pocket, he said he knew he didn't really need to stop doing coke but that I just needed to *feel* like he had stopped, and that in itself would make me happy. My father took me aside one day soon after and told me this: The things you do in your twenties are just things you do. But as you approach thirty what you do starts to become who you are. And there are some things you do not want to be forever.

I had signed my first book deal and secured a modest advance that wouldn't pay for more than a few months' rent, so I left Brooklyn. The new owners of our building were desperately trying to get tenants out so they could turn the building into high-end condos, so I took a buyout; moved to my parents' house in Woodstock, New York; and lived there for nine months as I finished my book and awaited its release.

Since then I've had people ask how I quit cold turkey—the drugs, especially. The truth is that I don't know. But I'm sure it's a lot easier when you have a nice roof over your head and work that you love. As my dad would say, it's not digging ditches. It seems strange to me that it was as easy as it was. Sometimes I wonder if I never turned that switch off completely and it's still there, waiting.

Because the truth is that up until a few years ago, I could not even drive through Williamsburg without my palms getting sweaty, thinking about how much I wanted to call my old dealer, still listed in my phone under the contact name "Coke." I don't know why I never erased it—it's been nearly a decade and I can't imagine he has the same number. But when I see the name and number with the rest of my contacts under the Cs I don't delete it; having another life—or the opposite of one—at the tips of my fingers feels comforting somehow.

I was dating again on the last day that I saw Ron. I was seeing a few different guys—guys who woke up at eight a.m., went to work, drank a few beers in the evening, and called it a day. Normal guys. Stable guys. Guys who answered the phone when I called and showed up to dates on time. One was so normal that I remember saying to my friend, concerned, *He wants to talk things out all the time.*

After we had sex next to a pile of dirty clothes on his bed that had been there since we first met, my distance must have been palpable. He was still naked as I started to walk out the door to go home. *I think I'm ready to move in together,* he said. Six months earlier this had been all that I wanted—some sort of recognition that what we had together was real and not just a drug-induced haze. But it struck me as so cruel in that moment—a way to keep me hanging on for just a few more months. I don't remember what I responded, just that I said it from the hallway.

D

DOING THE RIGHT THING HAS NEVER COME EASILY TO ME. I
cheated on almost all my boyfriends with regularity and without
remorse. I lied to my parents about failing out of my freshman
year at Tulane University, choosing to tell them that I wanted
to transfer rather than disappoint them with the truth. I don't
believe that right and wrong are black and white.

So when a close friend, a married friend, suggests he wants
to fuck me I'm surprised to find that I am not flattered. Still, I
tell him that I am. Despite my feminist bluster, I am the kind of
person who hates to say no or to disappoint. I would really like
for you to like me.

When a stranger on the street says something sexually
shocking, you can curse him out or keep walking. There are
fewer options when it's someone you host for brunch. Someone
whose wife you like and whose sons play with your daughter.
Someone who calls himself your husband's friend.

So when D messages me that there was a moment almost a
year ago at a book party when he felt the overwhelming desire

to be with me—and that this feeling has stuck with him since then—I'm not sure what to say. To make matters worse, he tells me this a half hour after I've taken an Ambien and the screen is a bit fuzzy and I wonder if I'm really reading what I'm reading.

But I do remember the moment he's talking about. I was wearing a crop top and a high-waisted skirt, so that a small sliver of my upper waist showed. I was glad to be out of the house, and glad Layla was spending the night with a babysitter so Andrew and I could have a fun night out in a city that we didn't know all that well.

A few drinks into the party, I snuck out with D to have a cigarette—a half cigarette, really, the limp last vice of boring married people. While we talked, he briefly put his hand on the exposed part of my waist. He stood closer than he should have and said we should sneak out for cigarettes more often. He had always been a flirt. Months before this, when I told Andrew that D kept looking at my breasts when he got drunk, he thought I was imagining it.

You think everyone is looking at your breasts! he joked. This is true.

D is well-known in his field and good-looking. But he is not someone who oozes sexuality. I was not remotely interested. Yet when he started to message me online not long after that party—it began with a note about a dress I wore at an event: "way to bring your A game," he said—I didn't tell him to stop.

Somehow, miraculously, my propensity for self-destruction did not win out, and I did tell Andrew about the messages. He wasn't pleased, but the come-ons were innocent enough that we could choose to see them as an idiosyncrasy—he was flirtatious. Big deal. It became a joke between Andrew and me—D as the inappropriate uncle or friend who gets handsy when drunk.

The truth is that we liked him.

We liked having friends with children. We liked having friends in Boston. It was easier this way. When D messaged me about a photo of myself that he liked or sent a random compliment, I tried to change the subject. I asked how his wife was. Were they still coming to dinner next week? I did act amused, though. I did say thank you.

But when he tells me about this moment he first decided that he wanted me, tells me that wanting something different is like an itch he needs to scratch, I am terrified. I erase his messages moments after reading them—as if my deletions can will them into nonexistence. I don't tell him to fuck off or to stop, though. I write that I'm flattered but what he's saying is dangerous. That our families are friends. Earlier this same evening he emailed Andrew and me about bringing a cheesecake to dinner at his place the following weekend.

I don't tell Andrew that night, but I can't sleep. So in the morning—to remedy whatever sleeping-pill-induced nonchalance I may have relayed—I write D a clearer message: I do not want to keep things from my husband. I need to be around your wife and not feel terrible. He apologizes profusely, says he was drunk and that he is mortified. I believe him but wonder if I had answered differently if he wouldn't be saying these things now.

Still, to my great shame, I want to make him feel more comfortable. I tell him it's fine. That I'll think of it as a drunken compliment and we'll leave it at that. I do not feel complimented. I would really like for you to like me.

I struggle for days over whether to tell Andrew: I know it is the right thing to do, but I also know that it will mean losing our friends and I don't want to cause a fuss. I am afraid of what he will think. But still, I can't sleep.

I can't figure out why I'm so distressed. He apologized, I had no interest—I could leave it at that.

But it occurs to me that D said this thing not because he was that drunk or to get it off his chest, but because he must have thought I was open to hearing it. That maybe I would respond in kind. He believes I'm the type of person who will dirty-talk with you online and then show up at your house days later to present your wife with a fucking cheesecake.

So when I finally tell Andrew, I can't stop crying. Not because I'm upset that I waited days to tell him and not because by telling him I know we are losing friends. I'm crying because I am thirty-three years old and I can't escape the feeling that men see that I am the kind of person for whom doing the right thing does not come easily.

It's why they approach me on streets or in bars or through messages on Twitter. They see me as the worst version of myself, the version I've worked hard not to be—or at least not to display too often.

I realize that I wasn't alarmed by D's first messages to

me—the seemingly innocuous ones about a dress or a photo—because the primary way I am used to communicating with men is through some form of flirtation. It did not feel immediately wrong or abnormal for him to be saying these things to me because these are the things that men say. And I cannot believe that so long after I first experienced a man making it clear that his desires trump my comfort, I still accept it. The only thing that gives me some hope is that I'm talking to my husband about it, about the way it makes me feel disgusting and cheap—even though it was not me who said the cheap thing.

I ask D to get a drink with me and tell him that I think he is blowing up his life—that you don't say something like this to someone so close to you unless you want to get caught, unless you want something to go wrong. He talks about the stress of his job and life, and I come to see this was never about me—not really. That his messages had nothing to do with his smelling my moral ambiguity a mile away gives me some comfort.

Still, I feel like I have done something terrible. As if I have betrayed D rather than the more solid truth that I have done the right thing. For everyone.

After decades of life and feminism, I still somehow believe that my job is to protect men at all costs—and that not doing so is a crime greater than keeping secrets from my family. Doing the right thing has never come easily to me.

ANON.

I DON'T REMEMBER THE FIRST TIME AN ANONYMOUS MAN TOLD
me to go fuck myself or said I was a cunt. I know it was probably
by email, since social media wasn't in full swing in 2004 when I
started a blog. I remember the first time I called the FBI, when
a man wrote us a few years after we launched to say that he
wanted to rape us and cut our breasts off.

I remember that I thought about what his real name could be.

I suppose these kinds of men have always been anonymous,
since even before the Internet. The men on the subways, the
men calling from their cars or the streets—the man whom my
friend Christine caught taking pictures of her exposed back
on a hot day when she decided to wear a sundress. The police
told her there was nothing they could do—taking pictures of
people's bodies in public isn't illegal. Even if they do plan to use
them to jerk off afterward.

We don't know who they are or how dangerous they are or
what they really want. We don't know, but we presume, that

they go home to families at night. Families with children, wives, mothers. Families with people.

On the street, as a teen, I learned quickly how to act. How to react. I don't believe that this is just a thing that girls in New York City learn, but I do imagine that we are advanced students in the topic. I knew, based on what time it was, what street I was on, and how many people were around, what I would say when a man would inevitably tell me on my way to school that he wanted to fuck me. Women know that this sentiment isn't always expressed audibly; men can say it without words, just with sounds, hand gestures, and facial expressions that stick with you the full day after you see them.

Talking back becomes a game of strategy. Figuring out if it's safe, or if there are enough people around, and if those people care enough to intervene if the man you want to talk back to decides to follow you or get violent.

I started off timid, nervous, and unsure. I shook my head, frowned, walked to the other side of the street or avoided their gaze. I walked faster.

If they followed I would go into a bodega or walk up the steps on a stoop, as if I was going home and there was someone waiting on the other side for me. The longer it went on, though, the angrier I got.

I tried shaming them: I'd ask them if they would say these kinds of things to their mother or their sister. Sometimes it worked but I stopped asking this question when one day, after I asked a man who said something about eating out my asshole if he had a daughter, he replied: *Yeah, and I'll fuck her too if I want to.*

That's when I started just giving the finger. Didn't look up, didn't break stride, just left my middle finger up and out and kept walking. No one tried to hurt me, which was lucky. I keep reading about women who get killed for the things they say to men on the street. Women who refused to hand over their phone number or declined propositions. A man in Queens who slashed the throat of a twenty-six-year-old woman who wasn't interested. A woman in Detroit with three children who was shot and killed after she refused to give a strange man her contact information. These two acts of violence happened within days of each other.

I have rejected men and I am okay, though sometimes I wonder how much that has to do with ridiculous, extreme luck and privilege. Once in New Orleans—as a seventeen-year-old freshman in college—on Halloween I dressed up like a "sexy nurse" and a boy kept following me and then started yelling things from the street below to the balcony I was throwing beads from, calling me a bitch. I told him he probably had a tiny dick. The crowd beneath laughed around him.

His face turned a deep red and he said, *I'm coming up to find you*, and I mocked him further. *Go for it*, I said. *I know your dick won't weigh you down.* Sometimes I wonder what would have happened if I had come face-to-face with him after that.

I think about the young man who killed people in Santa Barbara because he thought it unthinkably unfair that he was still a virgin and that beautiful women didn't want anything to do with him. Before going on a shooting spree he made YouTube videos about "slaughter[ing] every single spoiled, stuck-up, blond slut" he saw.

Still, somehow, inexplicably, "man-hater" is a word tossed around with insouciance as if this was a real thing that did harm. Meanwhile we have no real word for men who kill women. Is the word just "men"?

We say "misogynist"; I've written that "misogyny kills," but the word falls flat on your tongue—it's too academic sounding, not raw or horrifying enough to relay the truth of what it means. Besides, there are plenty of misogynists who don't kill—more than I'd like to think about.

Sometimes we call these men domestic abusers when the victim is someone they know, but when they kill strangers to them we just call these men crazy. Lone wolves. Unbalanced. But here's the thing—what is crazy about killing a woman in a culture that tells you that women's lives are worth nothing?

Women are raising children, picking up socks, and making sure you feel like a man by supporting you when you need it and looking sexy (but not trying too hard, because that would be pathetic). We're being independent and bad bitches while wearing fucking lipstick and heels so as not to offend your delicate aesthetic sensibility, yet even just the *word* "feminist" pisses you off. How dare we.

Still, no name for the men who kill women because we have the audacity not to do what we're supposed to do: fuck you, accept you, want you, let you hurt us, be blank slates for your desires. You are entitled to us but we're not even allowed to call you what you are.

When the words and threats come into your inbox or onto your timeline, assessing the danger is different. You don't know if the person behind the *cunt* or *you need a good dick* is a teenager who is showing off—though teenagers are capable of hurting women too—or if it's someone you know or someone who will show up where you work to get a better look. Once someone left a comment under a picture of a meal I made for my daughter that called me a bitch, and when I went to look at the man who had said this, the profile picture showed the hairless chubby face of a boy, thirteen years old at the most.

I have become too exhausted with men online to interact with well-meaning information seekers in real life. I get to speak to students, tell them about my work. Always, without fail, after the talk is given the first question is asked by a man. The first question is always some version of "What about me?" Ignoring men—whether romantically or rhetorically—is existential violence to them.

When my daughter was one year old some men decided to do a podcast about me, "revealing" who I am. The death threats started coming and so we left our house for a little while and stayed with friends in Manhattan who happened to have an extra bedroom. I knew these men's names, the ones who incited the threats. The ones who made videos of groups of them chanting about not wanting me to suck their dicks, as if that was the most offensive thing in the world to me. But their lack of anonymity didn't help me—I could report them to the authorities, and I did. But some men, men who have names, are careful. They don't say outright, *You should kill her;* they say, *I'm not saying someone should shoot her,* but . . .

It is easy to pretend this is funny. That it rolls off your back. Online especially, where sexists misspell regularly and sound ridiculous and silly. And so I will answer your obnoxious tweet calling me a whore or a cunt with a GIF of Jennifer Lawrence giving a sarcastic thumbs-up. I will mock your misspellings; I will make a joke of them. Because it's what people want to see— that you can handle this hate in stride.

In the same way that as a teenager I knew what men liked and became an expert in feigning whatever it was that they wanted to see, now I do the same for everyone else. You perform your strength, your sense of humor, your personality so that it is palatable, easily consumed in small, sweet, bite-sized pieces. The Internet is good for that.

PART III

It is the same woman, I know, for she is always
creeping, and most women do not creep by daylight.
—Charlotte Perkins Gilman, "The Yellow Wallpaper"

FAKERS

BY THE TIME I GOT CAUGHT WRITING NOTES SIGNED WITH MY mother's name to give to teachers after I had cut class, I had perfected both of my parents' handwriting. But my mother's—the messier of the two—was easiest. I practiced their names and certain phrases—*please excuse Jessica, feeling ill yesterday*—in spiral notebooks for pages on end. My mother, forever snooping for evidence that I was having sex, found one of the notebooks and confronted me.

It was bad enough that I had written notes using my parents' names, but my mother also found pages where I had practiced the signatures of my boyfriend's parents. So I wasn't just grounded for a month but needed to call Jay's parents too to apologize. I don't remember what I said to them, just that I was mortified, and that I continued to write notes anyway to get us out of class until Jay graduated at the end of my sophomore year of high school.

My signature today looks a lot like my mother's did back then—big, loopy, and illegible. So when I find myself sitting at a table after having given a speech at a college, signing my name over and over in books I have written, I can't help but cringe a bit at the mess I have left on the page.

Before I walk onstage to be on a panel or give a speech—a fortunate and strange part of my job—I say two words to myself internally: "slow," "smile."

I write the same words in the margins of my notes, so that while I'm speaking I don't forget to slow down my natural New York/Italian-American cadence and so the smiling calms me. It has the added benefit of making me come across as funny! and relatable! rather than angry, because for a feminist, anger is forbidden. It gives your opposition too much ammunition, even if you have every right to be angry and even if the stereotype should be long gone by now.

And so I smile and speak slowly (for me) and get to do something that a lot of people would love to do—to say what I think and have people listen to me. It is easy for me to say that to give a speech to young people and have them ask me to sign their books or take a picture with them is humbling. It has the benefit of being true. It's humbling, wonderful, flattering.

But the thing you're not really supposed to say because it sounds tone-deaf or ungrateful is the thing that sticks to the back of your brain and stays there: that being known by strangers is uncomfortable. And that I don't like it.

Or that you can come to like it too much. That the line of people waiting to talk to you can come to feel commonplace and mundane in a way that people sharing their stories with you should never be. But when you do something often enough, it becomes muscle memory. You sign books, pose for pictures, and answer the same questions at different colleges with strikingly similar auditoriums.

When girls tell me that a book I wrote made them a feminist and they want to hug me, I let them, but I also hate myself a little bit because the feeling I am feeling most is that if they really knew me they would never say that. But I say, *Thanks, thank you, that means a lot to hear, thank you.* It starts to feel like nothing, which is fucking horrible, because when someone calls you a cunt it sticks. It's everything else that feels like the fluke.

I am not supposed to say that. Of the horrible things that men say to women online, I am supposed say, *You get used to it.* Or *They must have sad lives, I feel bad for them.* And it's true—I imagine these men who spend so much time hating women and sending me pictures of fetuses or making videos screaming about my sucking their dicks must have sad lives. Of course they do. There is no version of a fulfilled life that allows someone to write *fuck you cunt* on Twitter or tell you over email that your four-year-old daughter will grow up to be a bitch like her mom.

But despite my best intentions and pseudo-Buddhist upbringing, I don't feel bad for them. I don't feel compassion. I just hate them. That's all I have.

I know I'm meant to be the bigger person; I know you're not supposed to hate people because hate is bad for your soul. But so is getting called a cunt every day for ten years. So is knowing that every time you produce something to put out into the world someone will try to kill it. That whatever you work on, whoever you are, the nameless horde of random people who go home at night and kiss their wives and children would like for you to disappear.

And that sometimes you want to, too.

Edgar Allan Poe once called the death of a beautiful woman "the most poetical topic in the world" and I've often found myself wondering how many woman writers who have killed themselves or let themselves be otherwise obliterated were trying, somehow, to fulfill this most popular of narratives. We're most valuable when we're smiling, dead, posing, our words hanging on the page with no real body behind them.

I'm supposed to say that *it goes to show we're making a difference* if we're making people that mad, and that's true, but what is also true is that it is terrifying. I don't want to give speeches anymore; I don't want to stand in front of a crowd because I am more afraid than I used to be. But still, I speak deliberately on that stage and I smile.

The first time I realized I was out of my depth was at a conference in Cambridge for women in the media on the MIT campus where the organizer opened the session by talking about the amazing women they had participating. She mentioned my name, in a room full of women, and a girl sitting in the row in front of me said, *Exciting!* My friend and I looked at each other, shocked. We knew that people read our website but it was hard to imagine those people reading our words as people sitting in front of us.

The best and worst advice I ever got about being powerful and having a successful career was *fake it till you make it*. So many of us, women especially, don't feel confident or worthy or smart enough to be in the rooms that we worked hard to get to. So instead of letting that insecurity take over and showing the world just how vulnerable we feel, we're supposed to act like we belong. Feign the entitlement that seems to come so easily to our male peers.

I live this advice every day and hate myself for it most of the time. *Fake it till you make it*, but at what point are you just a fucking faker?

The feminism of the day says we need to lean in and stake out our claim and not be shy about our accomplishments, but it wasn't so long ago that taking up any kind of space was considered feminist blasphemy—a thorn in the movement's side. When I was pregnant with my daughter, just starting to show, I was asked to take my name off the website that I founded and built. Not entirely of course, but the hope was that in sisterly solidarity I would disappear myself from a section of the site where writers could promote themselves as speakers. And I wasn't asked as much as I was shamed in the language of "collective leadership" and "feminist dialogue" to step aside by a person who could financially afford to do as much.

Succeeding as a feminist meant that you had failed somehow, profoundly, as someone who cares about other women. A *real* feminist shouldn't be able to make a living, have her work recognized, take up space. But the problem is that you already feel so small you don't think you could shrink down any more without completely ceasing to exist. But maybe that's the point.

The moments you feel large are fleeting—you blow yourself up but the air leaks out at a continuous rate as you speak and by the end of your sentence you're catching your breath again. *Slow. Smile.*

The first time I heard my writing read out loud was the same year that I got caught writing fake notes from my parents. My sophomore-year English class had been taken over by a substitute for the remainder of the semester after our original teacher left midyear. Mr. McCourt had retired from Stuyvesant some years ago but was funny and had an Irish accent, so everyone loved him.

I wrote about meeting my boyfriend's parents for the first time and getting caught, later, with the pages filled with their signatures. The writing assignment was anonymous and so he didn't say my name but as soon as he started to read and I knew the paper was mine, I wasn't as nervous as I thought I would be. I was thrilled. To hear my words in someone else's mouth, to see him speak them in front of other people, made me feel as if I existed.

It was the first time since I started at that school that I felt so out of place in that someone had picked something of mine, that someone had picked me. And so the following year I started to take creative writing classes and Shakespeare classes with the thought that they were similar to the acting I was already doing after school and couldn't believe my luck when my homework was actually just writing things down. Writing down anything I wanted.

I wrote about my parents, I wrote about boys, I wrote about parties, and one day when I got back a ten-page creative writing assignment from a teacher who was not Mr. McCourt, in the margins of a scene where I described my father yelling at me the teacher wrote: *Is he mad about your promiscuity?*

I am tired of faking confidence or being told that my lack thereof is a fault when it seems to me the most natural reaction I could possibly have to the lifelong feedback women are given. I don't want to be confident or inspirational and I don't really want to buck up anymore because the faking takes more energy sometimes than the work itself.

But still. The faking is what got me here. Every time I put on a sheath dress and heels and blow-dry my hair to go to a party or an "event" where they inevitably serve salmon, which I fucking hate, I feel out of place, because who the hell do I think I am, but also proud, because I am here. I like to send pictures to my parents.

A young activist who saw me at a fund-raiser once tweeted out, angrily, that I looked like I belonged there—among these rich people and well-coiffed pro-choice donors. As if fitting in was a betrayal, even though it's what I worked so hard for.

On my thirty-sixth birthday my daughter presented me with a "book" she had written because she wants to be a writer, like me, she said. The book, written on construction paper in crayon, bound together by string, was about watching me give a speech.

I was accepting an award from a humanist organization and Layla sat in the front row, avoiding her salmon but excited about the chocolate cake with the raspberry ganache, looking at me. She watched me talk for a while and didn't say much but wrote this book and drew the award, a placeholder for my confidence with my name etched in glass, proving I'm actually here.

We drove to Sesame Place after the event and watched as Layla avoided the people dressed up as the show's characters— *They're too big*, she said. *Are they real life?*

A few months ago, I gave a talk at a college, even though I had been sick for a few weeks. I felt weak. I smiled, and posed, and sat down to sign books afterward. But in the middle of the line at some point, when a young woman put her book in front of me, I signed my mother's name.

HANDS

THEY CALLED IT AN EMERGENCY C-SECTION BUT STILL FOUND
the time to shave my vagina. The nurse—I think she was a
nurse—used a blue Bic razor, the kind my mother would buy in
ten-packs and keep under the bathroom sink. I made fun of her
for using such cheap razors, embarrassed by her leg stubble and
bikini-line razor burn. I made a joke to the woman wielding the
razor across my pubic bone about not being well groomed—
Who waxes while pregnant anyway? She said nothing, left a few
red bumps, and was gone.

Three days earlier I had gone to my doctor for a checkup but
felt something was off and told them so. Layla's heartbeat was
fine but the nurse kept taking my blood pressure. Once, twice,
three times. Then my doctor came in, shut the lights off, and
told me to relax and lie on my side before she took it for the
fourth time. Then she had me walk across the street to the hospital.

I had never liked being pregnant. I felt more sweaty than
glowy and didn't appreciate the sudden willingness people

seemed to have about touching me: my stomach, even before it swelled; my shoulder, as if in commiseration. Overnight, strangers felt entitled to know if I'd be breast-feeding or to ask why my stomach wasn't bigger at six months along. *Are you eating?*

The first time I was hospitalized I didn't saunter over but was taken by ambulance after crashing into a tree with my back while skiing. I was fifteen years old, on a school trip, and was a moderately good skier. Still, on the first run of the day I hit a patch of ice and lost control. I saw that I was going to hit the tree and so I threw myself onto the ground, sliding down on my side the last few feet before impact. Later the doctor would tell me that this probably saved my life, or at least my ability to walk. I was lucky, they said, to have only ruptured my spleen and bruised my kidneys.

I was alone when it happened, and lay there in the snow for a while before a school friend passed by and went to go get help. Then two men strapped me into a sled and asked me questions about the date and my name. I must have gotten something wrong, though, because they called on their walkie-talkie for an ambulance.

I didn't have a bruise or scratch anywhere on my body, just a bad pain in my left shoulder. The strange thing, I told the doctor at the lodge, was that I hadn't hit my shoulder at all during the fall. That's when he told the man standing next to him, *We need to get her onto the ambulance now*. Apparently shoulder pain is a sign of internal damage.

My parents were a six-hour drive away at home so when

we got to the emergency room I asked someone to please call them for me. They let me get on the phone with my father as they worked on me, the coiled cord stretched tight to reach me in the gurney on the other side of the room. I told him I was fine but as we were talking a nurse put a catheter inside of me and I screamed. It was the first time that I cursed in front of my father.

I was able to avoid surgery to remove my spleen because the organ was encapsulated, they said, by a thin layer of skin holding it all together—keeping the blood from pouring into my abdomen. A few days later, whenever I shifted my weight, I could feel the blood sloshing about inside of me.

Fifteen years later, when my ob-gyn sent me to St. Luke's–Roosevelt Hospital, then in Hell's Kitchen, I was not alone. In addition to Andrew, my mother was with me. By pure luck she had gone with me to the doctor's appointment that day because Andrew had gone out the night before and was too hungover to drive. And so both of them were there with me as the doctor told us I would not be leaving the hospital until I delivered. My due date was three months away.

They said it was preeclampsia—high blood pressure, something that sounds innocuous but in pregnancy is deadly. A nurse put in an IV line in case I started to have seizures and they needed to get medicine into me immediately. We were skeptical, thought it was a fluke or my anxiety playing games with my blood pressure. I was healthy; I felt mostly fine. But with every new visit from a new doctor or nurse came more bad news.

After the first doctor said I wouldn't be leaving until I delivered we started to plan for how I would spend the next three months in the hospital. Andrew made lists of DVDs he could bring for my laptop, started to enlist friends to visit and bring food from outside of the hospital, and made a schedule of visitors on a spreadsheet. They kept testing my urine for protein, making me hold a pan over the toilet before I pissed so they could check it every time I went.

A neonatologist came into our room to tell us all of the things that can go wrong when you have a premature baby. We didn't understand. *I thought I was going to be here for three months.* She told us she would be happy if I could last another week before delivering.

I lasted three days.

Andrew's parents flew in from California on a red-eye and when I saw them I remember I cried and apologized; I'm not sure for what. The next day, they moved me to a different floor—a sign that I wasn't as urgent as other women who needed to be in the labor and delivery ward. But later that night they changed their mind and moved me back. Andrew's parents brought me a chicken dumpling soup from a nearby restaurant and I asked the nurses for an Ambien. A few hours later I woke up with horrible pain in my side and back. It wasn't just preeclampsia; I had HELLP syndrome: hemolysis, elevated liver enzymes, low platelet count. Or in layman's terms: I was fucked. I needed to deliver or risk dying.

Once your pregnancy has gone wrong—really wrong—no one quite prepares you for the sheer number of people whose hands will be inside you within a matter of hours. First, my doctor—no longer my original ob-gyn but a younger woman who was on call, whom I trusted immediately, maybe out of necessity or because of the fact that her fingers were touching my cervix. Then a man I had thought was an orderly but who turned out to be a doctor came into my room, lifted my gown, and shoved his fingers so hard into me I screamed. At least the anesthesiologist didn't finger me, but he was cute.

When he came into the room, despite the fact that I was swollen with fifteen pounds of water and had an on-its-way-to-failing liver, my sister and I found the time to exchange glances at each other with raised eyebrows. He had dark skin and gray eyes and he towered above us. I smiled and moved my hair—which hadn't been washed in days—to the side, behind my ear. I asked him if it would hurt.

Soon after a nurse gave me a drug to induce labor and I got to feel twinges in my stomach that they told me were contractions but just felt like jumps. I was glad to feel something. I hadn't felt the baby move much during pregnancy, just blips and here and there. Only one time, a few days before I got sick, did I really feel pregnant—the top of Layla's head poked up through my skin and Andrew and I watched, amazed, as it moved across to the other side of my stomach.

Within an hour of giving me the drug they said vaginal birth couldn't happen, my liver was in danger. And so someone shaved my vagina.

Andrew tells me now that my arms weren't strapped down,

but that's how I remember it. My arms lying out in a T shape weighed down by wires and tubes, being wheeled into a room naked from the waist down while handfuls of people prepared surgical instruments and talked to each other as if I was not in the room, my freshly shorn sad vagina on display.

My mother says that when she had a C-section she felt nothing; the family joke was that when the doctor asked how she was feeling—as they were cutting into her—she said she had a bit of a headache. But I felt everything. Not pain, exactly, but tugging and pulling and the shifting around of things that I imagine were my organs. I wondered if they were taking them out, placing them on the table beside me. I thought about what they might look like.

Andrew breathed in my ear what I'm sure he thought were soothing deep-breath sounds I was supposed to imitate. I just wanted him to stop but didn't say anything because I thought if I died, I didn't want to die giving him a hard time for being a good husband doing the best he could. I asked how much longer it would take.

I know that the doctors brought Layla to me for a moment after pulling her out of my open abdomen, before they rushed her to the neonatal intensive care unit. But the drugs I was on erased that from my mind. I fake a memory of it, so I have something, but the last thing I remember is starting to fall asleep while their hands were still in me and Andrew asking if that was okay. *She's probably pretty tired,* one of the doctors joked, and we both thought he was sort of an asshole for it.

Layla was high up in my belly so the doctor told me afterward that they had to cut me both ways, horizontally and vertically, and that because of this I should never have a vaginal birth in the future because contractions could make my uterus rupture.

And so I threw myself onto the ground, eyes closed.

THE BABY

THE FIRST TIME I REMEMBER SEEING MY DAUGHTER SHE WAS A picture of a baby that didn't look like a baby. A neonatal nurse brought the photo to me as I lay in the middle of a window-less recovery room after my C-section, separated from other women by a few curtains and a haze of drugs and exhaustion.

I held the photo—decorated with a pink printed border like something you'd get at a mall photo booth—with both hands. She was two pounds of red wrinkled skin hanging off tiny bones covered in tape and tubes. LAYLA VALENTI was printed at the bottom in script, the lettering blocking whatever machine was pushing air into her lungs. I was pleased that they left off Andrew's surname—a just mistake given the circumstances, I thought.

Before they brought the picture in, I kept asking Andrew what her name was, so I was glad to have the photo to remember. I asked for less pain medication so the confusion would let up, but the nurse said that wasn't such a good idea and gave me another two large round pills. When my mother came into the room, I waited for Andrew to leave and told her I thought

I was going to die. My body was too swollen with water for the nurses to draw blood—every time they tried they left an inch-deep indent in my arm—so they brought in an anesthesiologist to try to find a vein. It took him more than ten tries and twenty minutes.

I met the baby twenty-four hours later, lying on a gurney. A nurse wheeled me into the NICU and placed me alongside her incubator. I still couldn't sit up so I reached my hand through the hole in the plastic and used one finger to stroke her small red arm. A neonatal nurse told me preemies didn't like that, though—too much stimulation for something that was supposed to be in your uterus for another three months. And so I just lay there, looking at her—blue from the lights meant to help with her jaundice, a piece of foam tied across her eyes to protect them. She was on her stomach and moved her legs occasionally; it looked as if she was trying to climb or crawl away.

I held on to my stomach and wailed to my husband once I was back in the room that I needed my baby but stopped soon after, embarrassed at the display. Still, I felt empty—as if my guts had been left on the operating table.

When I was well enough to get my own room they wanted me to pump my breasts right away. Even though the baby couldn't eat yet, her digestive system too immature, they wanted me to start filling the NICU fridge. They gave me bags of two-ounce plastic bottles that attached to the bottom of my yellow breast pump, but when I tried the machine the only thing that came out of my nipples was brown ooze and blood. Still, I pumped, bleeding, until my nipples were stretched to three times their size in the machine and, finally, milk came. I attached stickers with the baby's name to the bottles and put them in the fridge alongside rows of and in drawers with other babies' milk. The color of the other milk looked cleaner, not like mine.

I want to say that a week later I refused to leave the hospital, that I couldn't bear the thought of leaving her there. But the truth is that I just wanted to go home. On the day that I left her in a large room with a dozen other sick babies, I begged my doctor to rush the discharge paperwork so I could be in my own bed before evening. She looked at me strangely and said, *You know your baby isn't coming home for a long time, don't you?* Yes, I knew.

For eight weeks, Layla lived in a plastic box called an Isolette. It was clear on all sides so she was on display for the nurses should she need them, with holes in the sides for handling her without taking her out of this box that would be her home for so long.

Outside of pumping, there was not much for me to do besides sit beside her. Sit and wait for her to wake up, holding her arm—not stroking—through the plastic hole. Sit and wait until one of the nurses agreed to help me pull her out, untangling the maze of wires, so she could rest on my chest. As she lay there I would breathe in and out loudly, my chest rising and falling, whispering, *Strong lungs, strong lungs.* But she could only stay with me for short periods of time because she was too small to regulate her own body temperature and needed to go back into the warmed Isolette, which I thought was an appropriate name for a box that babies had to stay in by themselves all hours of the day.

Every day, I got to hold her longer and longer, but most times that I did her oxygen level would drop or her heart rate would drop, and though the nurses didn't run over, they did rush—scooping her off of me to tickle her feet or move her around to get her breathing again or her heart going at a better speed. She turned blue a few times while I held her, once so much so that the nurse tapped on her chest until she was pink again.

It was the way I was holding her, they explained. I had to make sure her head and neck were at the exact right angle to let air through—if her head leaned too far back she would stop breathing, and if her head leaned too far forward it cut off her air supply too. I didn't like holding her much.

When I sat with her sometimes I would take an accounting of her wires: multiple stickers attached to wires for her heart rate, another attached to her foot for oxygen levels, her arm held together with Popsicle sticks and tape so she couldn't rip out the central-line IV that went almost straight to her heart. On good days she just had a nasal cannula, on bad days—weeks, really—she had a CPAP machine breathing with her, the plastic stretching out her nostrils and rubbing parts of her face raw. Later, there was the feeding tube—sometimes in her mouth, sometimes up her nose. While there she had a blood transfusion, a collapsed lung, eating and breathing problems, but no surgeries.

We were very, very lucky, they told us.

The other babies in the room had parents sitting with them

too, sometimes only one. One baby had been there a long time—he was bigger than all the other babies but just couldn't seem to breathe on his own. Sometimes babies weren't there anymore in the morning but were too small to have gone home, and so we knew where they had gone.

The song most frequently sung in the NICU was "You Are My Sunshine." Every parent sang it a different way—faster tempo, stresses on different words. Andrew and I kept track of who sang it worst. But what was universal were the lyrics, which struck me as appropriate: *Please don't take my sunshine away . . . When I awoke, dear, I was mistaken, so I hung my head and I cried.*

Andrew and I had a routine. One or both of us would spend the day at the hospital. The few days I took off from going I made myself watch videos of her crying or being washed, until I would weep or my breasts would leak through my bra. Just punishment for someone selfish enough to stay home while her baby lay alone.

At night, we watched *Friday Night Lights* on Andrew's laptop, ordered dinner, and then would share a carton of ice cream. At eleven thirty p.m. or midnight Andrew would call the NICU to check on her progress and ask the nurse staffing her that night to please change the position of her head. Most of the babies lay on their stomach with their head facing the door and the direction of the medical staff so that if they were in distress nurses might see it on their faces. But because they lay there for hours and days and weeks, one side of the babies' heads would start to flatten out. Changing her position from time to time helped to at least get a symmetrical flattening on both sides. Toaster head, they called it on the online preemie forums I looked through.

We commended each other on the excellent job we were doing. But Andrew still could not bear to look at her when he visited, preferring instead to look at his phone while he held her hand. And I just wanted to keep up appearances and publishing article after article even though I was convinced she was going to die every day and went to a friend's book party when I still had staples lining my lower stomach. A famous columnist looked at me, horrified, as I tried to walk and nearly collapsed.

The baby got out exactly eight weeks after she was born, one week after my one-year wedding anniversary, and four weeks after Andrew's twenty-seventh birthday. She was four pounds.

I don't remember much after she got home. I remember her sleeping upright in a car seat because her acid reflux was so painful that if she lay flat she would vomit and wail. I remember the first night sleeping with my hand lying on her chest with the hope that if she stopped breathing I would feel it on my palm. I remember posing for pictures, smiling, and sending them to my family.

My meticulously scheduled 2010 calendar tells me that a few days after Layla came home from the NICU, someone from a visiting nurse service came over. I remember she praised me for having the baby in a wrap, *to encourage bonding*, she said. The day after that Andrew took a CPR class, learning how to revive a four-pound infant should she stop breathing suddenly—a requirement for any parent bringing home a baby this small.

The next week we had a pediatrician's appointment, a pediatric ophthalmologist's appointment, and an early intervention specialist come over. The week after that I had therapy, another nurse visit, and a consultation with a pediatric cardiologist, who told us, in a Queens office where there was a dirty orange cafeteria tray next to the doctor's desk, that the baby had a hole in her heart. That we should come back in a few months, that she might need heart surgery.

Then another doctor's visit, another eye exam for the baby, a few friends over for lunch, and a second opinion on Layla's heart. This time we went to someone at NYU who had the latest, the nurse told us, cardiac imaging machine. This doctor told us no, she did not need surgery, she didn't need anything. Maybe the hole closed on its own—maybe first doctor got it wrong. We didn't need to come back. The following day we went to a pediatric gastroenterologist because Layla could not keep food down and was shitting blood.

She was allergic to dairy, so much so that if I ate a cookie with butter cooked into it and breast-fed her, red streaks appeared in her diapers.

I don't remember being a very good mother.

When I was still pregnant, I had agreed to write a book about parenthood. And now, with a baby that I was sure would not live and the inability to leave the house for fear that when I did she would die without me near her, I had to write it. The advance was gone—spent on medical bills and specialists and to hold us over because freelancers don't get maternity leave.

And so I met with my editor, who pointed out that I did not call Layla by her name but only said *the baby* or *her* whenever I needed to.

The brain does strange things to protect us. I knew that I loved her, but there is a difference between loving someone and having the ability to feel that love. To be fair to myself I wasn't feeling much of anything, but to not feel the most powerful emotion a woman is ever supposed to have—for a baby that needs you to survive, something you brought into this world—is the absolute worst, because you feel like a failure on the most basic, human level. Sure, you can write books, but if you can't even love your child properly what kind of shit person must you be?

This is when I am thankful for technology. Because, years later, when I see the pictures I took of her during this time—when I watch the videos of me cooing at her and laughing—I realize that I did not let my full-body numbness catch on. I was good at pretending, or maybe I wasn't pretending and was too buried in my brain to realize it. The mother on these videos looks present and happy, clapping when her baby dances, kissing her on the stomach, and stroking her arm to help her fall asleep. I wish that I recognized or remembered her.

At least, though, Layla might.

ICE

A FEW MONTHS AFTER WE MOVE TO BOSTON, INTO A RED HOUSE that sits at the beginning of the curve of a cul-de-sac, I start to eat ice.

I have always liked to keep a glass of cold water nearby—on my desk while I work, on my nightstand while I sleep—and so I don't notice at first that along with sips, I am taking the cold oblong shapes into my mouth and rolling them around before biting, the shards hitting the insides of my cheeks with cold.

But soon I'm not just eating the ice along with my water, but walking to the freezer multiple times throughout the day to pick out pieces to chew on their own. It may be Andrew who first notices, the sound grating enough to keep him awake at night as we lie next to each other. Whoever it is who first takes note, though, the initial thought that goes through my mind is about Rebeca from *One Hundred Years of Solitude*, who ate dirt and plaster from the walls. I frown at the thought of how she ended up alone and grieving, holed up in a large house.

Layla was one year old when we got to Boston but looked

no more than six months. When I bring her to a new pediatrician near Boston Children's Hospital, the other mothers stare at her in the waiting room as she holds on to my hands and walks, laughing and chattering nonsense like some sort of baby genius. Andrew and I joke about it often—her smallness giving other parents inferiority complexes about their own normal-sized children, their not realizing how lucky they really are.

Her new doctor tells us that Layla is underweight and she is sent to a nutritionist, who "prescribes" her vanilla ice cream every day after dinner now that she's grown out of her dairy allergy. I put butter in everything she eats, smashing it into her mashed potatoes and mixing it in with spinach, even black beans. I keep food on me constantly—in my pockets and purses— putting something into her mouth whenever she will tolerate it.

As if in solidarity, I lose fifteen pounds during those first months in our new house without trying. I go to a doctor to find out why this could be happening, shamefully, because I am more concerned about my hair falling out than I am my shrinking size. I know, though, it's because I've lost my taste for food. Still, I tell the doctor I'm eating normally.

It isn't a conscious move, but I can only bring myself to eat once Layla is asleep in her room and I can step out onto our balcony overlooking the street to take two small hits off a joint. Only then am I hungry enough to order takeout for dinner, mostly Cuban or Chinese food that I eat in front of the television as Andrew works late. During the day I simply forget to eat, or don't want to, and instead drink water and eat ice.

My doctor looks at the thinning hair at my temples and glances at my chart in her brown folder. *Two milligrams?* She's surprised at the amount of antianxiety medication I'm taking and wonders, she says, if the hair loss is just the result of stress. *Do you pull at it?*

Still, she's not happy about the pills. One milligram in the morning and one milligram at night. Despite the strict schedule, I carry the bottle of Ativan with me everywhere I go just in case I start to believe Layla is dead in her room or, like I did in New York, won't leave the house for fear that the moment I do something terrible will happen to her.

Our house in Queens—on a landmarked block in Sunnyside Gardens where every house has a backyard that melds together into a large common space with a weaving path—was old but huge. Three stories plus a basement where we put a Ping-Pong table. The neighborhood was one of the first planned communities in the United States, built in the 1920s; after the Great Depression more than half of the residents lost their homes. Rather than moving out, however, they mobilized, lobbying state officials, and when that didn't work they went on a group strike for lower mortgage payments. Most still had to leave.

While I was pregnant, we thought we wanted to live in this neighborhood of large trees and backyards permanently, and decided one day to look at a house for sale just across the shared common lawn behind our home. The couple who lived there were a decade older than us and had modernized the house beautifully: central air, a refurbished basement, an all-new kitchen.

The three stories were narrower than our own house but better maintained, and the rooms were impeccably decorated and colorful.

When we asked why they wanted to move they looked at each other first before answering that they just felt they needed a change.

We walked up to the second floor and in addition to an office space and long hallway, there was an empty bedroom—the only empty room in the house. It was pink with white trim at the ceiling and floor. On the back of the door and on the inside of the closets there were small white hooks screwed in just about at my hip's height. I immediately felt shame over telling them about my pregnancy, about how we wanted to buy a house to start our family in.

After Layla was born, this couple would enter my mind at inopportune times: while I was breast-feeding, while Layla was sleeping with my hand on her chest.

She was so small when we brought her home from the NICU that when I breast-fed her I had to be careful that while she sucked my nipple didn't sink into her face, covering her nostrils and smothering her. I was sure if I looked away my breast would kill her and I pressed the top of my areola with one finger as she ate to keep the skin away from her face. I'd let it go, to check—yes, it would kill her—and push it back in again.

Layla was so tiny that when I burped her, her whole body shook, her thin arms involuntarily shaking upward with each beat. When I look back at photos that I posted on social media at the time, I understand now why few people liked them: she did not look like a happy, well baby. She didn't fit into any baby swings or the car seat unless we padded the sides with rolled-up towels. We kept a spreadsheet of how much she ate and how often. I looked at her shits to make sure they were normal and that there was no visible blood.

Because we didn't have a baby shower for Layla—I was in the hospital about to have her by that point—relatives and friends kindly mailed us packages of welcome-home presents. Some toys, a high chair, and the smallest clothes they could find.

One relative sent a shirt-and-pants set from a company that specializes in clothing for preemies. Underneath the tissue paper, sitting on top of the tiny shirt with carrots printed on it, was a card advertising the company website. At the bottom of the card it read, "Bereavement sets also available."

I started to forget things. I'd be walking to my parents' health food store on Queens Boulevard—their latest small business attempt—and couldn't remember why I was going. I'd be talking with Andrew and ask him a question that he'd answered just minutes ago. One day, a bad day, I got into my car and suddenly realized that I was deep in Queens, driving through the neighborhood that used to house my parents' clothing shop when I was a child. An hour had passed that I could not recall.

When I looked at Layla I saw a baby with pieces missing. If I was on one side of the living room on the couch and she was in her swing on the other side of the coffee table, I couldn't see her mouth under the shadow of the blanket covering her and I thought it was not moving as she took in breaths. When she slept beside me in a small co-sleeper that attached to one side of our mattress, I woke up in the middle of the night and didn't see her legs there and jumped up for fear that they were caught in the sides of the co-sleeper or somehow, strangely, just gone.

The same thing will happen in Boston after the marathon bombing—I'll take Layla to the park a few days later and be shocked to see a three-year-old amputee at the slide, only to realize moments later that her body is, in fact, intact.

It is now, with the memory lapses and blackouts, the visual tricks and nightmares, that I realize there has always been something wrong with me. That this was always in me, this ability to disconnect without much trouble. I know I am living in the same world as everyone else but also feel, acutely, that I am living in a completely different one as well, all by myself. I am alone with Layla in the house most days and go without talking to other adults until Andrew comes home. I take walks to the park with her and point out the ducks but am mostly silent otherwise.

In the end, the doctors tell me I am iron-deficient anemic and I imagine that my veins are filled with something closer to water than blood, thin, cold, and motionless in my arms. Even though I am still not hungry, I start to cook every day with the hope that doing so will inspire me to eat. Butter-filled meals for Layla, elaborate short rib and pasta concoctions for Andrew and any guests who happen to come over. I bake cheesecakes and lemon bars with cups of sugar and whole sticks of butter but still they taste heavy and limp in my mouth. Nothing fills me.

I know I should not be this thin and I hate the way my breasts look deflated and stretched, but when I see my family and friends back in New York they keep telling me how good I look. *So skinny after a baby, wow!* Friends on Facebook comment on my cheekbones, suddenly more visible than ever.

I decide to stop taking my Ativan, which has stopped working. I only notice the medication in its absence—I forget to take a pill one day and I'm sweating and feel sick to my stomach. And so my doctor makes me a calendar of how to withdraw safely from this drug that doesn't work anymore, a calendar that takes weeks and necessitates a pill cutter, sleepless nights, and willpower I'm not sure I have. Smoking pot helps.

Around the same time Layla starts to talk in sentences, I start to gain weight. She goes to early intervention group classes in Boston with other children who were also born early or have disabilities. While there, if I wander too far from her side, she says, *Mama, here, Mama, here*, until I come back to her.

Later, when it comes time to drop her off there to stay without me, the teachers tell me she repeats this phrase over and over to comfort herself, now saying, *Mama's here, Mama's here*. She says it again at night in her room, the phrase coming through the baby monitor. If I don't go down to get her right away she starts to cry, then throws up. So I keep her in the bed with me and Andrew. *Mama's here*, I tell her. But I'm not so sure.

HOUSEWIVES

MY GRANDMOTHER STARTED DOING "FAVORS" FOR CASH SOON after her husband's moving business started to fail. My mother was a child, and she remembers the older Italian man who lived in their apartment building. My grandmother would walk up the stairs to see him, my mom says, and when she came down she would have cash in hand or there would be a little more food on the table that night. *It wasn't like she was a prostitute*, my mother tells me. My grandmother just knew she had to do what she had to do to keep the family going. Besides, my mom says, she doesn't know if she had sex with him or just gave him a hand job. Or if her young brain is misremembering. She does know that most of the money her mother got was pilfered from her father's pockets.

My mother was one of five children, three of whom she grew up with. Her second brother, Robert, became disabled after contracting a terrible case of pneumonia—the extent of which was never clear to me. He was in a wheelchair by the time he was ten years old and lived in an extended care facility after he turned fifteen, my grandmother pressured by her husband's family to move him there. Each week, for years, she would take an eight-hour bus ride to see him because of the lack of facilities nearby that she could afford. I found out about him as a teenager, when he died and she went to the funeral.

My mother was youngest, the baby, and though her mother was a housewife in the sense that she raised her children without much help from her husband and had food on the table every night, my grandma also worked ten hours a day for almost her whole life. She worked as a nanny, but mostly at factories, one called Goldsmith Brothers and another where she worked on an assembly line for a company that made airplane parts.

Her husband, Giuseppe—known in the neighborhood as Joe—owned a truck and a moving business. He piled the neighborhood children into his truck to take them to the beach on weekends, and my mother says that Joe hired men that no one else would—the men who spent all day in bars or black men who lived in the neighborhood.

It was the hiring of these men that my grandmother would blame for the failure of her husband's business. The clients didn't like seeing them, she would say. Not the fact that her husband started to drink in earnest, so much so that my mother would lock herself in a closet when he came home raging at night.

Joe died a few years after he and my grandmother split and many years before I was born. He set himself on fire after an accident with a hot plate in the apartment he lived in. He was drinking at the time. It wasn't the burns that killed him, though, but an infection he got later in the hospital. My mother tells me that after my grandmother developed dementia, she would call out Joe's name in her sleep or sometimes talk to him when she was awake as if he was there. She felt responsible for his death, she said.

I SMELL SOMETHING BAD WHENEVER I WALK INTO MY HOUSE. I don't know if it's the garbage can, or strong cheese rotting in the fridge, or flowers that have been left on the dining room table a few days too long. All I know is that something does not smell right.

Andrew gets furious at my insistence that something somewhere is going bad because he smells nothing and because I always seem to crinkle my nose when I come home from a days-long trip and he's the only one in the house. The smell wouldn't be there, he thinks I think, had I been home.

It probably wouldn't.

Not because Andrew is dirty or derelict in cleaning or being an equal partner but because my nose is so sensitive that I catch things early. Once when I was pregnant I refused to drink a glass of water that Andrew had brought to me because it smelled terrible. *Water doesn't have a smell!* he yelled, but still he got me a new glass because he is a kind person in that way.

Boston smells the worst. Our house in Boston, I should say. Despite the fact that we live in a large house—larger than any place we ever had in New York or ever will—the smells of the house carry through everywhere. I can smell the cat litter three floors up, or the dried puke stuck in the crevices of Layla's crib from across the room. I feel perpetually disgusted and clean constantly.

Every time I see a dirty cup on the kitchen counter, my face gets red. The level of disrespect feels—unfairly or not—as if Andrew has hopped on the counter, pulled down his pants, and taken a shit right there for me to clean up. My husband is lovely. He is a feminist. He cooks; he supports my work in the same way I support his. Still, I start obsessively making mental lists of the things Andrew doesn't know: what size shoe Layla takes, when her next doctor's appointment is, what kind of bar soap we use in the shower. I'm jealous that he gets to stay late at work—I would kill to have an office, coworkers, even a commute.

He tells me to leave the cups on the counter and the socks on the floor. He'll get to them eventually. But I can't. I don't believe him. And I can't write in a house where something is wrong.

It may be genetic.

When I was growing up there was a running joke in my family that you could never put something down—a magazine, a set of house keys, a glass half filled with soda—because the moment it left your hand my mother would "clean it up." We would scream at her, my father, sister, and I, that we couldn't find anything in this fucking house because she kept putting things away.

The house wasn't just clean but immaculately clean. Everything had a place, and everything had to be in its place. Friends who came over were amazed to see this gleaming, well-decorated house in the middle of our shit neighborhood. Even more so when they went to get themselves a snack. My mother kept the fridge so stocked with food that I often couldn't close the door without shifting things around. Our cupboards—tall doors that opened to reveal layers or swinging shelves within— held dozens of boxes of pasta and canned food. Ten different kinds of cookies, cereal, and snacks.

My father told us it was because of how little food my mother had growing up; she just wanted to be surrounded by it. To know it was there.

Layla can't really breathe in Boston, as if her lungs can sense the same thing that my nose does. We're taking her to the emergency room every couple of months when she starts to breathe too fast or when her cough just won't stop. Our insurance company won't cover the cost of a vaccination that preemies are supposed to get to prevent RSV—a lung infection that can be deadly for babies born so small. We call the company directly, hoping just to buy the vaccine from them, but the shots cost four thousand dollars each. She needs five of them over the course of the year.

Even after Layla is rushed to the hospital after contracting RSV, unable to eat, sleep, or breathe normally, our insurance company says no—her death needs to be imminent, they tell us.

And so I drive Layla to New York, where her old pediatrician keeps some of the medication for those who can't afford it in a fridge in the back of his office, and he gives her the shots as she wails in my arms. This is why I will always prefer Queens to any other place—the borough of my parents and small business owners is populated by people who know how to work around the system when it tries to fuck you.

When I arrive home in Boston, opening the door with Layla balanced on my hip, the smell is there again, but this time I can't find it. There is nothing in the fridge; the garbage has just been emptied. I even go to the side yard and clean up any leftover dog shit from our Aussie, Monty, with the hopes that it will make a change. I can't sleep that night even when I put a pillow over my face to mask the smell.

Andrew and I have been going to couple's therapy, both for my anxiety and because Andrew is so mad at the space the anxiety takes up in our relationship. Our default mood is low-level annoyance toward each other with a propensity to turn into full-blown rage at the smallest thing: his clothes on the floor, my refusal to make a salad with avocados in it. The therapist asks if I would be less resentful if Andrew did more around the house, asks him if he's willing to speak up for himself more often.

I feel like I might hate him and I suspect he feels the same. He doesn't believe, not really—not yet—that my PTSD is a thing out of my control. He says lots of people feel things, it doesn't mean you let everyone else see it. It doesn't mean you can't make it stop or that your whole life has to revolve around it. I accuse him of being an emotional robot; he accuses me of using my anxiety as an excuse to be selfish.

Some months later we are in a session devoted to the way that my post-traumatic symptoms impact our relationship. The therapist wants to do something called EMDR, a kind of therapy that utilizes rapid eye movement to help a patient with a particularly bad memory or event. When she hands me a laminated list of "negative connotations" and asks me to pick out the one that I most identify with, I am surprised when I start to cry because the one I choose is *I deserve to die*. No, not surprised. Embarrassed maybe. It feels too performative, this sentence on a list of sentences, and yet I pick it anyway.

I don't talk with Andrew about it again.

MY MOTHER HAD LESS TIME FOR THE HOUSE ONCE MY GRAND-mother got sick. She still kept it gleaming, that's true, even as she worked all day and then cared for my grandmother after work in the evening and on weekends—bathing her or taking her to a doctor's appointment. But she was around less, and even when she was home I knew her thoughts were elsewhere.

My sister and I tried to visit my grandmother as often as we could, on the eleventh floor of an old-age facility in Astoria where there were pull-cords to ring for help near the tub and the toilet. The apartment was filled with glowing paintings of Jesus and pictures of her grandchildren. It smelled like piss topped with the compact powder she used to blot oil from her face.

When she needed to go out—for an appointment or a family party—my mother would sit with her and help her "put her face on," tracing over her eyebrows with a pencil and then filling in her lips. My grandmother would remark, often, how glad she was that she never really had wrinkles on her face. It was true, she didn't—but only because the majority of the loose skin was hanging below her neck, as if her face had melted a bit.

She got confused easily and started to make mistakes around the house: accidentally brushing her teeth with vaginal cream or feeding her dog shampoo instead of washing him with it. She left messages on our answering machine claiming that the woman who came to help her wash up was a lesbian who "wanted her pussy." She became convinced, toward the end, that strange men were following her or waiting outside of her apartment door in the hallway.

My mother started going over more and more often but wasn't there when she died. Her makeup looked wrong in the casket—too heavy and pink for her face. I couldn't smell her powder, just the thick recycled air of the Long Island City funeral home.

CHERRY

SCOOT DOWN.

The feminist who gets one abortion is understandable, expected even. The woman—the mother—who gets two, though, must be doing something wrong with her life.

Still, I scooted.

For a body that cannot abide pregnancy, mine sure does like to get knocked up. It's as if my body wants to kill me—filling me with something that I'm supposed to love but will end me instead.

The weekend that I got pregnant again we spent on a speedboat. The condom had broken the night before we were supposed to drive to a friend's house on Long Island—we talked about picking up the morning-after pill on the drive over, but the traffic was bad and we just wanted to get there. *It's okay,* I said. *It will still work in twenty-four hours.* So fucking smug.

I hated the boat. Our friend Josh was perfectly competent and in control while driving it, but still I grabbed on to anything that looked like a handle and wrapped my legs around Layla as if she would go flying off the back of the speeding boat at any moment. She kept wriggling away from me, her white-blond hair in her face, laughing and screaming. *Wheee! Faster! This is fuunnnn!*

I thought about what I would do if she fell off the back of the boat. She would probably be okay, I reasoned, because the boat was going fast enough that the motor would be far away from her. But then I thought about her small body and the motor and closed my eyes. I imagined jumping off.

Josh pulled close to a small beach so we could take a swim break and his two boys jumped in without hesitation. We weren't that far from land so I eased my way into the water. *Hand her to me*, I told Andrew. *I can swim her to shore.*

I propped Layla on my hip, she wrapped her arms around my neck, and I started to sidestroke. Two minutes in I started to feel winded. Layla climbed up higher on me, pushing her feet down into my stomach. I told her to relax, that we were almost there, but she kept pushing. Her feet were under my ribs now and I felt myself sinking lower and lower.

I thought about drowning. How I could probably hold her up for someone to grab as I went under. How she could be saved, even if there was no way I would be. But everyone would say how brave I was.

But my toes hit rocks and I could put my feet down onto the ground, and I made it to the sand, winded but fine, and Layla ran to collect shells and chase birds.

A few weeks later, I took a pregnancy test without telling

Andrew—no reason to worry him, I thought—and when it came back positive, I wailed. Layla ran over, asking what was wrong. She had never seen me cry before, and certainly not like this, sitting on the bathroom floor loudly weeping. I told her I was fine, smiled I think, and picked up the phone. She, unsure, laughed.

Andrew was home less than an hour later, my mother not far behind. Andrew and I left the house and went to get patty melts at a place on Smith Street two blocks up from the Brooklyn apartment we'd just moved into. He said all the right things, carefully, but I knew what he wanted me to do. Our marriage had barely made it through the two years after Layla's birth— through what it did to me, through Boston—and that time we were lucky. That time we had a baby who lived through it all. Layla was healthy now, hadn't had a hospital visit in almost a year, and we were finally back in New York. Still, we went through the motions of doing the logical things you're supposed to do.

We made appointments with specialists, talked to family and trusted friends. I cried. The funny thing about pregnancy is that with any other health risk a doctor has no problem telling you what the best course of action is. But no doctor will tell a pregnant woman what to do.

You could do it, they say. *But yes, the HELLP could come on within twenty-four hours, and your liver could fail.*

We would watch you, they say. *But we can't stop you from getting sick.*

We don't know what will happen to the baby.

And so for a week we keep talking and seeing doctors. Because we have just moved back to the city, I don't have a regular ob-gyn. So I go to a doctor I have never met before and she gives me an ultrasound as I weep while telling her about my last pregnancy. As I recount the hospital stay, the NICU, my blood pressure and liver count, she turns the ultrasound screen away from me. She lowers the sound. But still, I see the flicker on the screen.

That day, a week after I take the test, I tell Andrew I want to end the pregnancy. He tells me he knew I would come to the right decision, that I had to get there myself. And so we make an appointment at the place I know. The place I have been before.

MY BODY HAS NEVER PLAYED NICE. WHEN I STARTED TAKING THE subway in junior high, I noticed that when I held on to the handles above me or the pole in the middle I only leaned to one side. I could jut my right hip out, putting most of my weight on that side, and have space between my waist and hip to rest my hand. But when I tried to do the same thing on the left side of my body, there was no hip—my waist and hip bone met straight on, with no curve.

The doctor had me bend over in front of him, pulled my shirt up toward my neck, and felt up and down my back. He told my mother it was scoliosis and that there was probably nothing to do as I'd stopped growing, two years after I'd gotten my first period. Still, my parents took me to a specialist they said was very good because he was in Manhattan and affiliated with a hospital. I got undressed for the X-rays, save for a gown that I wasn't sure how to put on because I didn't know which way the opening was supposed to face.

The pictures came back immediately and the doctor showed my mother how I had two curves in my spine: one at the top near my shoulder bones that was slight, and one at my hips that was nearly at a thirty-degree angle. It explained my inability to lean but one way and the pain I got in my back if I stood for too long, sat for too long, or slept for too long.

I was too young to appreciate the medical reality of this news but knew that I really, really liked my X-rays. You could see the outline of my breasts—which I thought looked good—and in my skull you could see my earrings and a piece of gum that I'd forgotten to take out of my mouth before placing my back against the machine. I asked to keep the images and the doctor put them in a large brown envelope for me so I could take them home.

Sometimes, when boys I liked were over at my house, I would show them the X-rays under the auspices of how funny it was that I had gum in my mouth, but really it was to see their reaction to the image of my tits, even if it was just the outlines.

Now, in my thirties, I wonder if the scoliosis is the reason I'm so clumsy—if I'm somehow off-kilter and that's why I keep banging into things as I walk around the house or why I've broken the same pinky twice already from stubbing it too hard.

I wake up with bruises that seem to have appeared out of nowhere, like they did in my drinking days, but I'm not drinking. Not sleeping either. When I take Ambien, or melatonin that I get from my parents' health food store on Queens Boulevard, I mostly sleep through the night, but still get up to piss at least four or five times. My doctor says don't drink water before bed but still I get up. Sometimes when I wake I stay that way and watch as Andrew and Layla, who has come into our bed in the middle of the night, sleep and it occurs to me how different they are from me.

And so I walk through the apartment, or I sit on the living room couch looking obsessively at real estate listings on Zillow for houses I will never live in, until I'm tired enough to try again.

ON THE MORNING OF THE ABORTION THEY CALL ME WITH THEIR address—a fact held back nearly a week for security purposes and one I don't remember given the years gone by. But I do remember that they were in midtown somewhere, on a high floor of a nondescript building, more office space than clinic. Just like last time, I am the only person there. This time it's over a thousand dollars for the privilege of being alone. I wonder if they remember me. After my book was published a few months after my first abortion, I sent them a copy with a thank-you note—they had helped to make that book happen.

Like before, it is more midwifelike than a hospital—from the tea to the candies and the hand-holding nurse with the soft voice. But that doesn't stop me from crying when the doctor tells me they no longer offer IV sedation, just a single Vicodin I know won't make a dent. World's worst combination: a low tolerance for pain but a drug addict's tolerance for painkillers. Still, I take the pill, hoping that maybe I'm wrong this time.

I wish I could say that it hurt less the second time around— that the knowing what to expect helped. But I did not want to be there.

I hated myself for waiting a day to take the morning-after pill. I hated Andrew for not having to do a goddamn thing but sit there at my head pretending he knew what it was like to have people doing things to your body, inside your body. He didn't know shit.

When I was in the thick of it with Layla's birth there came a point where I tried to convince the doctors not to deliver her— even though every moment I delayed I got sicker. *Keep her in*, I said. *I don't matter.* But as I begged them to keep her in, my body worked harder and harder to get her out.

Now, once again, my body ignored my wishes. It clenched and held on even as I assured the doctor that this is what I wanted. It fought me, trying to hold on to this pregnancy, this pregnancy that could be a baby that could be a death sentence, this pregnancy that could be.

I did not give in but the pain of the procedure overtook me. The speculum felt high up in me, cold and hard, and the pain emanating from my vagina into my abdomen felt like I was being skewered. The nurse at my side told me to bear down as if

I was having a bowel movement and that would help relax me, and it did, but it still hurt so much. I start to see double.

I felt pins and needles in my face and hands. Andrew looked alarmed, and I heard the doctor say it was all over and she came to where my head was. *Get her legs up,* she told the nurse. They lifted my legs, like dead weights, above my head and the nurse pressed wet paper towels onto my forehead and wrists.

They said I had a lower pain tolerance than most—*You're so sensitive!* I lay there, waiting for the warmth to come back to my face. And it did. My breath became slower; I stopped crying.

The doctor went to the sink with what she had pulled out in the syringe and looked for proof that it was all there. Andrew tells me later that when they were done looking, they washed what was left down the drain.

Slowly, I was able to sit up, Andrew still at my side. The wet brown paper towels are sticking to me; my pants and underwear are on a chair nearby. I feel better.

My daughter is waiting at home for me. My mother is with her and will stay a few more hours as I crawl into bed and settle in with a heating pad and painkillers. I think I'll feel well enough to cook with my daughter, keeping up our weekend ritual of making pasta from scratch that we'll cook with tomato sauce.

Before I leave, the nurse asks if I want a candy. I picked cherry.

CHOCOLATE

LAYLA DREW A PICTURE OF HERSELF ONCE THAT SHE WANTED ME to hang on the top of her preschool cubby for all of her friends to see. It showed her—blond hair, green eyes, a body drawn in red crayon—with four words beneath her feet: *I am shy. Layla.*

"Shy" is the word we use with her; "mutism" is the word her therapist uses.

Layla's hope was that by putting this picture and declaration where all of her friends would see it, they would understand, just a little, why she doesn't talk to any of them. Not to say hello, not to say thank you, not a word. Just silence.

Sometimes, when she is feeling jolly, Layla will make hand signals to her friends, nod *yes* or *no* or make clicking or whistling sounds when she wants someone's attention. To her best friend, the girl she is most comfortable with in her class, she will mouth sentences.

Most days, my daughter chatters away with me, telling me about school and her best friend—*I love her so so much, Mommy.* She talks about her imaginary friends: Super Bad Guy Snowmen who litter our street with ice that makes it difficult for her to walk. She tells me about her boogers, her poops, her toys, and the dreams she has at night (ladybugs on beaches). Sometimes, she wakes up laughing—not giggling, but in fits of hysterical laughter. She can never remember what was so funny in her dream.

I've come to believe that the hours of silence she endures in school make it so that by the end of the day she is desperate to get her words out, sentences flowing into each other without stopping. She has always been articulate, ahead of other children with when she began to speak and the kinds of words and complex sentences she could put together at an early age.

That is why, when she was two years old, in day care but not speaking to other children, we didn't think much of it. It made sense to us that she only talked to the teachers; her friends weren't even putting sentences together. She told us this directly when asked why she wouldn't talk to her friends: *They don't know how to talk, Mama.* And so parental pride blinded us.

When she was three and still silent we chalked it up to the gender breakdown in the class—mostly boys, loud and exuberant. Layla was still very small for her age and preferred quiet play so again, we didn't worry.

But when she was four years old and in a quiet and supportive Quaker school, Layla told us she couldn't talk to other children that she had known for months because when she tried, it felt like she was meeting them for the first time. She told us she was too afraid.

The diagnosis was selective mutism—an anxiety disorder in which children will go mute in certain settings or with certain people. For Layla it means she will only talk with adults, no children, and only those grown-ups whom she knows and likes.

It is difficult to explain the strangeness of never having seen your daughter speak to another child.

Once or twice she has forgotten her rules for herself and slipped up, saying a word or two. When her father and I have joyously pointed out these occasions she's gone mad, insisting that she never said anything. That we imagined it or the words were meant for an adult in the room. She does not waver—whether it's out of fear or an unwillingness to believe she is capable of speaking, I don't know.

She has friends; for that we are grateful. Her friends know Layla doesn't talk but that doesn't stop them from jumping on her bed during a playdate. Little girls whom she holds hands with and hugs, one little girl who writes her love notes day after day with their names in hearts together. They tell each other *I love you* by pointing at themselves, then making a heart with their hands, and then pointing at the other person. If they are feeling a lot of love they will end the hand sequence by holding their arms out wide so as to show the depth of their feelings.

To see your child who has so much to say go silent at the sight of a friend is just pure pain. To watch her create her own sign language to help her communicate rather than use her voice is terrifying, because you can't help but think of things to come—some silent future where she cannot stand up for herself or, worse, adequately express her joy. And while other five-year-olds are kind and understanding, children do not stay that nice for that long.

And so you do what the specialists tell you to do, all the while knowing that this is a thing that you passed on to her—not the silence perhaps, but the fear behind it. That your genetic propensity for trauma and anxiety is the only thing she got from you. Everything else, everything good, is her father's. Her blond hair and green eyes that make strangers believe you are the nanny rather than her mother, her intelligence, her humor, and her curiosity are all characteristics you find unrecognizable in yourself. The worry, though, you recognize.

When Layla was born, I had this feeling that she was not really mine but all Andrew's somehow. As if I could birth a child that carried no pieces of me. But now, with this, I know she is so much mine, and for that I wish I could tell her I am sorry.

Sometimes I hate myself because I want to scream, *Just fucking talk I know you can do it*, because I cannot understand how it is possible that she literally cannot get the words out. But then I see her cover her mouth with her hands at even a kind suggestion that she just try to be brave and I know it's not just willfulness that's holding her back.

And so we bleed money for therapy that our insurance company won't cover—money for phone calls with teachers, travel time for her therapist to get from Manhattan to her school, check-in sessions with us. We create "brave talking" charts and collect prizes to give her when she speaks during a panicked moment. I scream at the big boys on the playground who bully my silent child while their asshole Brooklyn parents watch apathetically.

A friend gives Layla a "fairy door" for her birthday that we slide up against the wall and tell her will bring a fairy to her room while she sleeps. I write a note in crayon from the fairy urging her to be brave, attaching a small gold ring I wore as a child that I tell her is magic and will help her get her words out. She wears it on a necklace and one day she is able to say the ABCs to her teacher while looking at a classmate.

If Andrew and I have anything, it is words—sometimes so many of them we talk over each other in an effort to get them out. I have so many I need to take to paper every day. Sometimes I feel like I'm not really in a room but just floating smiles and words filling up the space around me.

Layla, though, is there. She wants to talk about how much she's growing, how much she weighs, how much space she is taking up. *Watch me dance, watch me clap, look at this sweater I have—it's pink!* When we are with my parents in upstate New York she brings me sage leaves from my mother's garden and instructs me to smell them and to rub them against my face.

We travel to California for Thanksgiving to see Andrew's parents, taking her out of school for two weeks to play with her grandparents in their yard with lemon trees, sew outfits for her dolls, and delight in the small army of rubber ducks that line the bathtub in my husband's childhood home. There's a persimmon tree outside where crows pick at the fruits, thrilling Layla and terrifying me.

The first night we are there we go to a restaurant and, like her new therapist advises us to, tell her that she can have whatever dessert she wants if she can just order it from the waitress. She asks if she can look at me while she says the words loud enough for the server to hear, and I tell her, pained, that she cannot. I know she will just be pretending that she is talking to me.

As the meal goes on, Layla gets more jittery. She wants me to read her the dessert choices, and I do—they have an ice-cream sundae. She asks to sit on my lap and has me go over exactly what this might look like. *I will say, "Excuse me, miss, my daughter would like to order something." You just need to look at her and say two words: "Ice cream."* She shifts on my lap as the woman approaches. I ask the waitress if Layla can order something and her mouth moves but no words come out. I tell her she needs to speak louder.

She whispers, *Ice cream,* but too low for the waitress to hear. I tell her one more time, *You need to say it louder,* and as the words come out so does a choke of a cry as the waitress looks at us strangely and I yelp and hug her close. She reaches for her father and weeps, smiling, as the woman in the black and white outfit turns around to bring her chocolate ice cream.

ENDNOTES (2008-2015)

Fishy Cunt? Censor your smelly twat, not my free speech.
Email, April 22, 2008

———

You and your cult are the majority of the reason that women are hated. You can't tease the poor men and then yell at them for drooling. You don't see men walking around exposing bits of their private parts all the time and even if they did I would expect to see most women staring and drooling if they were attractive.
Email, May 31, 2008

———

GET BACK IN THE KITCHEN AND MAKE ME DINNER, BITCH.

Tiny brained women, why did we ever let them think they are someone?
Email, June 8, 2008

———

Your site is FUCKING BULLSHIT! Get in the kitchen where women should be and start cookin! No but on a serious note, you guys suck.
Email, November 6, 2008

———

Do my dishes and clean my house!!!!
Email, December 20, 2008

———

I looked at your photo, and I wasn't attracted. Why not? You are a fine-looking young woman. After a while of looking at the photo I realised why. You seem to have "sleepy eyes".

It is a fairly serious issue. I knew a man at work who had real "hooded eyes", his eyelids were half-closed most of the time, it looked really evil. A far more extreme case than your photo. To "take a good photo" is a skill learned by actresses and maybe you should learn it.
Email, May 12, 2009

———

fuck you fuck you

fuck you fuck you fuck you fuck you fuck you fuck you fuck you
fuck you fuck you fuck you fuck you fuck you fuck you fuck you
fuck you fuck you fuck you fuck you fuck you fuck you fuck you
fuck you fuck you fuck you fuck you fuck you fuck you fuck you
fuck you fuck you fuck you fuck you fuck you fuck you fuck you
fuck you fuck you fuck you fuck you fuck you fuck you fuck you
fuck you fuck you fuck you fuck you fuck you fuck you fuck you
fuck you fuck you fuck you fuck you fuck you fuck you fuck you
fuck you fuck you fuck you fuck you fuck you fuck you fuck you
fuck you fuck you fuck you fuck you fuck you fuck you fuck you
fuck you fuck you fuck you fuck you fuck you fuck you fuck you
fuck you fuck you fuck you fuck you fuck you fuck you fuck you
fuck you fuck you fuck you fuck you fuck you fuck you fuck you
fuck you fuck you fuck you fuck you fuck you fuck you fuck you
fuck you fuck you fuck you fuck you fuck you fuck you fuck you
fuck you fuck you fuck you fuck you fuck you fuck you fuck you
fuck you fuck you fuck you fuck you fuck you fuck you fuck you
fuck you fuck you fuck you fuck you fuck you fuck you fuck you
fuck you fuck you fuck you fuck you fuck you fuck you fuck you
fuck you fuck you fuck you fuck you fuck you fuck you fuck you
fuck you fuck you fuck you fuck you fuck you fuck you fuck you
fuck you fuck you fuck you fuck you fuck you fuck you fuck you
fuck you fuck you fuck you fuck you fuck you fuck you fuck you
fuck you fuck you fuck you fuck you fuck you fuck you fuck you
fuck you fuck you fuck you fuck you fuck you fuck you fuck you
fuck you fuck you fuck you fuck you fuck you fuck you fuck you
fuck you fuck you fuck you fuck you fuck you fuck you fuck you
fuck you fuck you fuck you fuck you fuck you fuck you fuck you

fuck you fuck you fuck you fuck you fuck you fuck you fuck you
fuck you fuck you fuck you fuck you fuck you fuck you fuck you
fuck you fuck you fuck you fuck you fuck you fuck you fuck you
fuck you fuck you fuck you fuck you fuck you fuck you fuck you
fuck you fuck you fuck you fuck you fuck you fuck you fuck you
fuck you fuck you fuck you fuck you fuck you fuck you fuck you
fuck you fuck you fuck you fuck you fuck you fuck you fuck you
fuck you fuck you fuck you fuck you fuck you fuck you fuck you
fuck you fuck you fuck you fuck you fuck you fuck you fuck you
fuck you fuck you fuck you fuck you fuck you fuck you fuck you
fuck you fuck you fuck you fuck you fuck you fuck you fuck you
fuck you fuck you fuck you fuck you fuck you fuck you fuck you
fuck you fuck you fuck you fuck you fuck you fuck you fuck you
fuck you fuck you fuck you fuck you fuck you fuck you fuck you
fuck you fuck you fuck you fuck you fuck you fuck you fuck you
fuck you fuck you fuck you fuck you fuck you fuck you fuck you
fuck you fuck you fuck you fuck you fuck you fuck you fuck you
fuck you fuck you fuck you fuck you fuck you fuck you fuck you
fuck you fuck you fuck you fuck you fuck you fuck you fuck you
fuck you fuck you fuck you fuck you

Email, August 9, 2009

———

Don't look so serious next time when you post your picture. I bet
you have a beautiful smile :)

Email, November 19, 2009

———

Hallo, I saw your videos at youtube. Never thought that a feminist could have such a charming smile and appear that friendly. What are those videos for? Greetings
Email, February 18, 2010

———

Sometime ago I sent you a message expressing some objections and some questions I had about one of your YouTube videos that I had recently watched at the time. It has come to my attention whilst cleaning out my inbox that you never responded and that saddened me a bit. It distresses me the see that after all that talk you did not reply and I assume it was due to lack of time or not getting the letter rather than lack of courage to calmly discuss your principles with an intelligent and verbose male.
Email, April 11, 2010

———

Jessica you are having a baby? I thought you didn't believe in having babies . . . just killing them. I feel sorry for your child who will learn to devalue human life
Email, May 1, 2010

———

You, Jessica, are the prototype bitter liberal woman in this article. One can only imagine the venom dripping off of your keyboard after you finished this angry screed.
Email, May 29, 2010

———

I had abortions because I thought it was a birth control option.
NOW I am a murderer, if someone is niaeve or cruel enough to
abort a sweet baby, they are uninformed or selfish. That's the
bottom line.
Email, November 10, 2010

———

So you pple do slut walk? Look at yourself, fat elephant, you
and the likes of you don't need to worry about getting raped.
In LA, you'd have to pay for that, dumb broads. Hope your
children will get violently, brutally raped. And yes, I'm a
feminist and female. Just the trash like you and your website is
polluting the movment and doing disservice, ugly fat pig.
Email, June 4, 2011

———

Looking over various photos of you something became startling
apparent. This is the most flattering and you are still homely.
Which begs the question—why are so many hardcore feminists
so unattractive?
Email, September 20, 2011

———

Show me a woman or girl, and i will show you someone with
issues. no respect for themselves and their bodies.
Email, March 15, 2012

———

I think you need to be gagged. All we do is fuck and chuck women nowadays because of the rhetoric of cunts like you. I hope you perish in a gasoline explosion induced car crash.
Email, April 11, 2012

———

I just read Full Frontal Feminism and it sucked! I am not a mysoginist or a hater. Your book just really sucked.
Email, July 27, 2012

———

It seems as if you are ungrateful. Everything is built by men. Men even invented tampons. Please grow up and become a lady rather than a little girl.
Email, July 28, 2012

———

Feminists remind me of little girls who cry because they didn't get their way. If you wanted to be important, you should have been born with a penis. (:
Email, August 8, 2012

———

You really do need psychotherapy. You need to explore your childhood and the effect your parents had on you.
Email, September 1, 2012

———

Do you see women overtaking control of men in years to come? I am curious . . . Please feel free to email . . .
Email, November 28, 2012

———

[Jessica Valenti] has achieved mainstream acceptance with her books and articles in the Washington Post and The Atlantic. Surprisingly, she got married, but to a man who was awarded a "beta of the month" prize. She was somewhat attractive for one picture in her life, but she looks nothing like that now.
"The Nine Ugliest Feminists in America," ReturnofKings.com, January 5, 2013

———

Your book is silly. And you are silly.
Email, January 10, 2013

———

@JessicaValenti: Twitter friends: Anyone know a country where tampons are free or somehow subsidized? 8 August 2014

@amcphee: @jessicavalenti I think she meant where they sell them oversized, for her giant gaping vagina

@skzdalimit: @jessicavalenti If you're so worried abt tampon availability, maybe U need 2 stick a few fingers in UR you-know-what to stem the bleeding.

@spergonwynn: @jessicavalenti cunt

@watchdougals: @jessicavalenti Yeah it's called the Middle East where they sew your vagina shut for being a loud mouth

@jhendricks2301: @jessicavalenti don't think it's on part to being stoned, do you if you can't afford tampons use an old fxxking sock

@bobolewsky: @jessicavalenti Why haven't you had your ovaries, etc. removed yet?

@mrsugarbutt: @jessicavalenti here's a thought: get married. Then your husband can pay for it. As long as your putting out . . .

———

You're one heck of a disgusting ugly looking hag. What you need is a big fat dick inside you to set you straight. Thankfully, you're nowhere near being my type. I hope some mack truck crashes head on into you.
Facebook message, June 30, 2014

———

Fuck you, you goddamn whore!!!
Facebook message, June 30, 2014

———

OINK. . . .
Facebook message, July 1, 2014

———

Care to be the first in line, stupid little girl? Get the facts straight. NO taxpayer and no business with a strict moral code (unlike you) should have to pay for you or anyone else's birth control. And yeah, you come to my local Hobby Lobby and try to demonstrate what a tart you are, spoiled little girl.
Facebook message, July 2, 2014

———

What you need is a vacation in Afghanistan. Where through a sniper's scope you see little girls raped, their their vaginas cut out, made to eat it then beheaded. If you want to fight for women's rights. GO There. Until then, SHUT UP.
Facebook message, November 7, 2014

———

There's no clear evidence on whether prolonged increases in testosterone over time can change the growth trajectory of bones enough to produce changes in face shape. But if true, it would go some way to explaining Guardian's Jessica Valenti's dramatic transformation in the last ten years.

"Does Feminism Make Women Ugly?" Breitbart, July 26, 2015

———

Tony B.—pretty lady

Mark W.—She doesn't look that bad there. How come she don't get catcalled no more?

Eric F. —She's not really that Attractive. BARF!!

Joao D.—I am sorry I can't see her as attractive the only thing I can feel when I look at her is rage and disgust

Tony B.—She's not GORGEOUS, no. But I think she's relatively attractive.

Richard J. (profile picture: baby in pumpkin costume)—She's fine . . . Of fuck, like you wouldn't . . .

Vasanth P.—The magic of makeup.

Scott B.—Sorry I find her physically attractive, however I can't get past that personality of hers.

Matt T.—I would. As long as I got to use a ball gag.

Brent B.—She has rat teeth.

Richard J.—I think she is quite beautiful.

Brent B. (posts pictures of his red and white cat)—Beautiful in the ass. Id give her in the d in the dumpster only. And I'd make her call me daddy.

Chris P.—I personally find black widow spiders beautiful in form and function but I would never cuddle up with one.

Daryl W. (from Alberta)—Moderately attractive brunette right up until the moment she opens her mouth to speak . . . . at which point she gets really ugly really fast.

Melissa L. (posts makeup tutorials)—looks like a snarky cunt just by the way she smiles . . .

James H.—This is before she gained weight. Now she looks very average.

Jon B.—I know most of us are not saying it but the sheer fact that not only what these feminists say by believe to the core makes up lose respect for these people, it reduce them to nothing but what they claim as being a sex object, but not at our fault but by their fault. Why because the only thing they become useful for at that point is a hump and dump situation. When you have nothing in common but sex it's not hard to do. People don't stop to think about when your core values suck it takes from everything you are!

James H.—Agreed. I would cum in Jessica's eyes. But only if it will cause an infection. Otherwise it just enables her.

James W.—man jaw

Thread on the "Honey Badger" Facebook page, underneath my author photo for this book, 2015

———

ACKNOWLEDGMENTS

As is the case with everything I write, this book would not have been possible without the support of my husband and best friend, Andrew Golis. Andrew, I am grateful for you every day.

To Mom, Dad, and Vanessa: Thank you for allowing me to use your stories, which are as crazy, complicated, scary, sad, fun, and amazing as you all are. I love you.

I've now worked on two books with my inimitable editor Julia Cheiffetz—I cannot imagine a fiercer advocate or friend. To my excellent agent, Laurie Liss, thank you so much for the unwavering support and making this book possible.

Juliet Critsimilios helped me in ways big and small, with both this manuscript and my very complicated life surrounding it. J, you are smart and funny and wonderful—I can't wait to see what you do next.

Layla, love: Everything I do—everything I write—is done with the hope that when you grow up you will be proud of me. (And not too embarrassed about the sex stuff.) At five years old you are braver than most adults I know, so I cannot wait to see the person that you become. I love you with my whole self.

ABOUT THE AUTHOR

JESSICA VALENTI is a columnist for *The Guardian* US, where she writes about gender and politics. In 2004 she founded the award-winning Feministing.com, which *Columbia Journalism Review* called "head and shoulders above almost any writing on women's issues in mainstream media." Her work has appeared in the *New York Times*, the *Washington Post*, *The Nation*, and *Ms.* She is the author of several books, including the national bestseller *Full Frontal Feminism*. Jessica lives in Brooklyn with her husband and daughter.